A message from the author:

WARNING!

Just reading this book won't help you or your business. You have to do something with it!

If you purchased this book:

Thank you! I'm honored by your belief that my book can help you. However, the warning above still applies. Putting a book on your shelf doesn't impart its wisdom directly into your mind. Read it. Apply it. Prosper.

If this book was a gift:

I hope you thank the person who gave it to you. What's the best way to thank them? Read it and let them know what you learned from it. Then show them what you've done with it. Sadly the overwhelming majority of free books never get read. I hope this one does, and I hope you pass it along for others to enjoy.

SOARING PRAISE FOR
CONQUER THE ENTREPRENEUR'S KRYPTONITE

"It's rare to come across a book that addresses planning and strategy that is so engaging and helpful. James reminds us how to make sure our goal is truly our own, identify fake obstacles, take action, and see our greatest potential released. With this book you can move from planning to seeing the results you've been dreaming of come into view."

– Dan Miller
Author of the New York Times bestselling
48 Days to the Work You Love

"A really great, well-grounded, easy-to-understand, practical and powerful guide to the basics of strategic planning. If you've never done comprehensive planning work, *Conquer the Entrepreneur's Kryptonite* is a solid place to start. If you've done it for years, I'm confident you'll come out of the book with a number of helpful tips and insights anyway!"

– Ari Weinzweig
Co-Owner and Founding Partner of
Zingerman's Delicatessen and Author
of A Lapsed Anarchist's Approach to
Building a Great Business

"Personal accountability is about owning our results. Entrepreneurs require a plan to achieve those results. James Woosley shows us how to create that plan using a simple, flexible strategy that drives purposeful, responsible action."

– John G. Miller
Author of QBQ!, Outstanding,
Flipping the Switch, and
Parenting the QBQ Way

"If we hadn't started strategizing about Saddleback Leather, a lot more cows would have died in vain. James is a planning stud and this book will definitely get you thinking about your business in ways you never have before."

– Dave Munson
El Presidente
Saddleback Leather Co.

"As a lifelong advocate, proponent, guide, and participant in self-employment, I can attest to lack of planning being an Achilles heel of monumental proportions. James has created something new; a planning strategy we can actually digest and implement. Yes, even for those of us who are planning averse and suffering from it. Thank you, James. Thanks for living it in your own life, and allowing us to benefit. You're the needed and wise 'safety' for my trigger-happy self."

– Kevin Miller
Founder, FreeAgentAcademy.com

"It's difficult to put *Conquer the Entrepreneur's Kryptonite* down without making something happen. This book is a must-read for anyone who hates the planning process but knows they need one."

– Justin Lukasavige
CoachRadio.tv

"Dreams and ideas and businesses don't just happen. They take a lot of hard work. That work is much easier with a plan. But many plans only make things more difficult. The Simple Strategic Plan outlined by James will equip you to make things happen, whatever your endeavor."

– Jonathan Pool
Strategist & Catalyst for Change
JonathanPool.net

"This isn't a book you read once. It's a guidebook you'll read and reread as you build plans to leave your mark on the world."

– Alan Jackson
PowerOfWHY.com

"If you want to be a successful entrepreneur, you have to be intentional and purposeful. *Conquer the Entrepreneur's Kryptonite* offers the plan and strategy to help you show up and shine."

– Kent Julian
Author and Speaker
KentJulian.com

"James has a unique ability to make difficult and boring topics (like planning and strategy) engaging, interesting, and easier to understand. More importantly, he helps you put it into practice quickly so you can take action in your business."

– Deb Ingino
Strength Leader / Coach / Mentor
StrengthLeader.com

"Wow, James' book is written with wisdom that makes sense for 95.43% of business owners. His real world simple models get the results you need without the complexity most plans seem to drown in. The first three chapters alone are worth it if you easily suffer from over-planning OR hate to plan."

– Christopher Browning
Marketing and Business Coach
BusinessSuperPowers.com

"James is the planner—the detail man that pushes everyone to new levels in mapping out their business, their message, and most of all their life."

– Jonathan Tollefson
PARXbyJonT.com

"The Simple Strategic Plan is a clearly-defined path that I can follow. It helped me to identify the steps needed to accomplish my goals with enough detail that I could actually 'see' my plan through to fruition."

– Melodie Kenniebrew
MochiInTheDesert.com

"When I thought about strategic planning I was thinking bullet points, deadlines, and sterile, bleached lingo. James uses a creative approach to provide a framework to document our plans and move quickly to actionable steps. If you are looking for a way to organize the launch of your business or just get new projects on track, look no further!"

– John DiMare
AwesomeImpact.com

"It is without reservation that I can say that the Simple Strategic Plan (SSP) was the key process that transformed my life. I was able to create a step-by-step plan to take me from having an idea to being a successful entrepreneur. The SSP moved me from being overwhelmed by distant, lofty goals to feeling excited and confident. I have successfully achieved my goal of self-employment!"

– Robert Coburn
Founder, Total Fusion Ministries
TotalFusionMinistries.org

"James is amazing in helping people understand how to create a plan. Using the Simple Strategic Plan helped my vision for my business truly take shape."

– Wendy Staas
NaturalBirthEvangelist.com
EmpoweredMothers.net

"The Simple Strategic Plan helps you break down a seemingly huge task into smaller, manageable bites. James' method also helps to organize your purpose and vision so you can focus on what's most important."

– Cindy Thomas
CindysVirtualServices.com

CONQUER
THE ENTREPRENEUR'S
KRYPTONITE

Simple Strategic Planning for You and Your Business

JAMES WOOSLEY

FOREWORD BY CHUCK BOWEN

Organize Chaos | Prioritize Focus | Get Stuff Done

FREE AGENT PRESS

Conquer the Entrepreneur's Kryptonite:
Simple Strategic Planning for You and Your Business

Published by Free Agent Press, FreeAgentPress.com
ISBN: 978-0615822907
VID: 20130920

Cover Design & Graphics by George Amequito, GeorgeAmequito.com
Edited by Jennifer Harshman, HarshmanServices.com
Back Cover Photo by Kerry Kruegler, KerryKruegler.com

To my grandmother, Marjorie Greer:

Because of you my dreams are bigger.

Thank you for always believing in me.

Contents

Contents

FOREWORD

There are a plethora of great books (in an equally abundant number of formats) on the subject of starting up, building, and growing businesses. My recent Amazon search on the topic of "business" yielded almost 6,000,000 search results; a "business planning" exploration gave me almost 91,000 results. "Simple business planning" coughed up just a tad over 500 responses; "simple strategic planning" gave me 275, less than 0.005% of all business-related media on Amazon.

Could it be that strategic planning ain't that simple?

From my experiences coaching hundreds of small business owners over more than a decade, that's what the vast majority (okay, all of them) would testify. Far too many entrepreneurial dreams have crashed and burned for lack of a solid, thoughtful action plan birthed from a mission and vision important enough to inspire confident steps forward.

Stephen Covey helps us get things done through balance (*First Things First*), John Maxwell guides us to be principled and influence others (*Becoming a Person of Influence*), Jim Collins shows us how to make the leap to greatness (*Good to Great*), Seth Godin implores us to lead (*Tribes*), while Tom Peters' *In Search of Excellence* (one of the most important business books of our time) reveals principles that made America's best-run companies the successes they are. These are absolutely must-reads, without question. However, who's going to show the small business owner the "how" (to plan and execute) behind the "why"?

*A plan, a plan, my business for a plan...**that I can work confidently!*** If you can make your business work on paper, you can likely make it reality. If it won't work on paper, what you have is a pipe dream. A "good planner" is one who creates a thoughtful plan. A great planner (with the bank account to prove it) not only creates his thoughtful plan...he ACTS on it.

In *Conquer the Entrepreneur's Kryptonite*, James outlines his SSP (Simple Strategic Plan) method for getting the right things done. "You don't need a business plan. You need a plan for your business." He begins with helping you learn why your mission must drive your actions.

Passion (from the Latin *pati*) means "to suffer." So, in more modern thinking, I define as passion "to care so much about something that you're willing to suffer with near infinite energy to achieve it." There have been very few who've been so passionate about planning that they're willing to suffer through, including myself. James is going to reveal to you how to simplify your planning, pump up your confidence, embolden your actions…while conserving your passion for *the* thing that truly matters—your business!

Good plans help us take responsibility for our results on paper before we have to do that in real life. So, in one perspective, plans help us live out our dream on paper *before* having to take the ultimate risk—doing it. A good plan ensures your mission is viable, not a slam dunk. It's good enough to pursue with everything you've got *and* make adjustments as you learn that things aren't going exactly like you thought they would.

"The concept of creating something alone and revealing it to the world is a lie." (*Conquer the Entrepreneur's Kryptonite, Chapter 1*). Influence for good, and seek to be positively and powerfully influenced by others. James will come alongside you to break it down into simple steps, and then put it all together to give you the confidence your business deserves…*and you dream of.*

Chuck Bowen,
Business Coach and Serial Entrepreneur

INTRODUCTION

This is a book for people with ideas. If you have lots of ideas (or just one really good idea), this is the book that can help you bring them to life. But you have to move beyond ideas and dreams…it's going to take a plan.

Do you make plans that never get implemented? Are they so complicated they fail because you simply can't make them happen?

Or do you resist planning because you just want to get things done, but end up failing and reworking things more than accomplishing your goals?

Let's find the happy middle ground, the sweet spot that combines planning and action!

What is it that you want to achieve? Whatever it is, it's not going to be easy. Not if it's something BIG worth doing right.

The goal is for this book to make it easier, and in doing so, make it look like it was easy to anyone who didn't see the blood and sweat you poured into your idea.

While it is written and addressed to the individual who wants to start a business venture or is already running a business, it can be used in a variety of ways.

It can be used by small teams to chart a course that uses everyone's input in order to get all the players on the same page (though it may require an external facilitator, even if there isn't already internal conflict).

It can be used by an individual who wants to organize and take control of their life. It's an excellent tool for anyone who has recently been through a LifePlan or other personal coaching process to capture decisions and structure follow-up actions.

It could be used by a family to structure their collective dreams and goals, and to help them support each other as they pursue them.

It could be used by an individual to structure their efforts for a job search, including doing a real evaluation of what kind of job you want instead of blindly sending out a thousand resumes.

It could be used by an organizational leadership team to manage significant change initiatives. [However, for most organizations or churches, I would recommend a more intense and comprehensive facilitated process known as StratOp[1]. You can learn about StratOp at WoosleyCoaching.com/stratop.]

Basically, it's for almost anyone that needs a plan more comprehensive than what fits on a napkin, but less complicated than a binder overflowing with pages of details.

What is the Entrepreneur's Kryptonite?

I will admit at the beginning of this book that I am not the world's biggest Superman fan—I don't dress up in tights or go to conventions. But I am a fan.

I grew up watching Superman movies and Justice League cartoons. But I didn't read the comic books and missed out on a very important part of the Superman story.

Kryptonite—the shattered fragments of his home planet, Krypton—isn't always green.

In its first appearance, Kryptonite was red. And through the years there have been many kinds of Kryptonite, with each version affecting the Man of Steel differently.

Somehow this otherwise invincible superhero has a weakness caused by a rock. It's kind of silly, but at the same time, it makes it easier to relate to him. He isn't a god. He's a man with special powers.

I have special powers. Seth Godin helped me discover that in his book, *Linchpin* (a must-read).

You have special powers, too! Even if we don't always know *what* they are, there are superpowers inside each of us. But those

---

[1] The Strategic Operations Plan (StratOp) process was developed by visionary business guru, Tom Paterson. The Paterson Center continues his legacy by training and equipping a growing community of facilitators of the Paterson Processes (LifePlan and StratOp) who guide individuals and organizations to discover and realize their missions and visions in life (PatersonCenter.com). I am a certified StratOp Facilitator.

powers must be discovered and exercised. They must be developed into true strengths we can use.

With great power comes great responsibility...and fatal flaws. Kryptonite. And just like in the lore of Superman, it comes in many colors.

For the entrepreneur—anyone with dreams and ideas they wish to share with the world—there are many kinds of Kryptonite. There are procrastination, pride, stubbornness, and many more. But there is one that arches over all of these Kryptonites. The big green Kryptonite for entrepreneurs is improper planning. Planning too little or too much opens the door to failure, allowing a flood of other types of Kryptonite into our lives. They choke our dreams and ideas. They keep us from using our superpowers to benefit mankind.

Kryptonite is real and cannot be banished from existence. But there is a solution. It can be controlled. It can be placed in a lead box so that its impacts are minimized.

This book will help you find the sweet spot between planning too little and planning too much. And when you can do that, you'll realize your superpowers and change the world!

My Story

Planning has always come easy for me. It's the execution and follow-through that prevented me from reaching my potential.

My mind is very logical and analytical. I'm a natural planner and creative problem-solver. Bring me a challenge and before you've finished describing it I'll already have several ideas in mind (and several that came to mind but I've already realized three steps ahead that they won't work!).

So how did I get to this point, writing a book on strategic planning?

It started from a very dark place in 2008. I was working for a consulting company on a very difficult project. The work environment wasn't very rewarding, and I had been passed over for promised promotions twice in two years. But in that dark place I was able to see the small spark that changed everything.

I had been teaching Dave Ramsey's *Financial Peace University* for several years, and through his radio program heard about Dan Miller's book, *48 Days to the Work You Love*. I didn't love my work at that moment, so I read the book. The Ramsey/Miller one-two punch was enough for me to realize that I didn't want to work 80 hours a week to become a partner in the company and make $300,000 a year. If I was going to work that hard, I was going to own the company! Owning my life was more important than the money.

Because of Dave's influence, I had started doing financial coaching, helping people pay off debt and build a financial plan of attack. Dave's Baby Step strategy clicked in my mind and I could translate the process to other people (even if I wasn't doing it fully myself).

At the same time, Dan was launching his own FPU-style course, so I drove to Nashville to get certified. I was nervous because even though I travelled 50 weeks a year for work, I rarely took a trip for myself. I'm cheap and rarely invested any money in myself. So I was uncomfortable and worried that this was just another boondoggle on my part or a scam on his part. Gladly, it wasn't anything like my worries!

Dan and his family treated me like family from the very beginning. I felt welcome and I was instantly more comfortable. Many of the people I met at Dan's home are still my friends today. They encouraged me and inspired me to join an online community that would eventually become the Free Agent Academy (founded by Dan's son Kevin Miller and Chuck Bowen). That was March 2009, just over four years ago at the time of this writing.

I started attending Free Agent Academy events in Tennessee and Colorado. I was so active in the online community and engaged at the live events that people thought I was an extrovert (I'm definitely not!). The passion for my future had been lit, but I still had no real direction. I was doing a lot of self-discovery exercises and evaluations, but I wasn't getting any traction.

That was a time of significant personal development, yet little growth. It was as if the seeds inside of me were planted and growing roots, but no sprout had appeared from the earth.

I have many people to thank for "feeding and watering" me throughout that time, but there are three key stories that I need to share about Chuck Bowen to help you understand my personal transformation:

1) The First Meeting:

I met Chuck at the first FAA event in June of 2009. Chuck is an incredible coach and has a reputation for diving deep into a person's mind and soul and making water pour from their eyes! He didn't make me cry at that first event, but he sensed the wall I was putting up and taught me how I was dismissing my own greatness.

When people would offer me a compliment, I would dismiss it by saying it was "no big deal." Not only was I missing out on the benefit of a sincere act of appreciation internally, I was throwing it back in their face. My attempt at humility was in fact self-destructive and hindering my ability to develop deeper relationships.

Through a little role playing, Chuck taught me how to accept a compliment and that doing so is a gift to the giver. Deflecting a compliment is rude; it's the same as throwing their gift in the trash as they look on, making them feel bad. It's best to sincerely accept the compliment and say how great it is to be appreciated.

It also pointed to some real self-esteem issues. I felt very egotistical on the inside, but I was dismissive of any and all earned honors and appreciation. I put down my greatest work, believing it to be inferior to what others could do, simply because it was easy for me (sometimes our greatest strengths are like that).

2) The 2x4 Incident:

A few months later, I flew to Colorado to attend another FAA event. This was the one where Chuck hit me between the eyes with a 2x4.

Okay, that's not what literally happened, but it sure felt like it on the inside!

After months of interaction in FAA, I was well-known amongst the leaders and the hundred or so members. They respected what I had to say when I offered my opinion or advice on their questions. Meanwhile, I was worried that I came across as a "know-it-all," especially at events when I seemed to have to hold back comments when others were telling their stories or trying to solve a problem.

Just before dinner one night, after I was sharing a bit of my story, Chuck looked at me and said, "James, you are the biggest underachiever in the room."

That sentence burned all the oxygen from my lungs. My heart stopped beating and there was no blood moving to my brain anymore. How could he say that? I was hurt and trying to understand what he meant.

Five minutes later we were in line for dinner. I was talking with him and said something like, "I don't know if I'm an underachiever. Sure, maybe I'm not meeting my potential, but…".

And he said, "What's the difference?"

At that moment it clicked. He wasn't putting me down. He was lifting me up. He was believing in me, just as everyone else in the room was believing in me. I had a gift I was using, but I didn't see it.

It was as if Superman was flying all over the place saying, "What? It's no big deal."

Dude, you're in tights and flying all over the place. It's a big freaking deal!

While it took a lot of time to process what I learned that night, it was the point at which I really did start to believe in myself.

3) A Strategic Realization:
In February of 2010, Dan Miller hosted his first annual 48 Days cruise. I was in full learning and buying mode now, so I jumped at the chance to spend more time with him and Chuck, as well as fellow coaches Justin Lukasavige and Kent Julian.

It was my first cruise and I went without my family, so there was a lot of quiet time to reflect. I'm not a morning person, but I was awake at dawn each day, energized to get going and growing.

I think it was the fourth day of the five-day journey when Chuck struck a chord with me again. He was teaching a session on strengths based on the research of Marcus Buckingham and Donald O. Clifton in *Now, Discover Your Strengths*, which was later refined by Tom Rath in *StrenthsFinder 2.0*.

I had already taken the StrengthsFinder exam and my top five were Futurist, Achiever, Relator, Strategic and Ideation. These concepts rang true, though I always wondered if Strategic was correct.

My background in the military meant I had a pretty solid connotation of the word strategy. It summoned up mental images of binders full of war plans covering every possible contingency. I just didn't see that in myself.

Yet there in Chuck's presentation was a chart I'd never seen (or hadn't noticed) before. It categorized the 34 Strengths into one of four domains. As I captured the chart's contents into my notes, I saw that three of my Strengths fell into the Strategic Thinking domain.

I was confused. I didn't see myself as a strategic thinker. But I didn't have a good definition of strategy, either. My mind was muddled with thoughts of military war plans and not open to much else.

As I talked with Chuck about it after the presentation, I realized that I am in fact a very strategic thinker. I could see threads reaching back in my life that served as further evidence of this truth.

Why did I like Dave Ramsey's Baby Steps? It outlined a simple strategic process to get out of debt and build wealth.

Why did I like Dan Miller's 48 Days process? It outlined a simple strategic method to finding work that you love.

Why did I overanalyze every situation I found myself in, paralyzed to move forward until I sorted through all the possible scenarios in my mind? Strategic thinking was working against me in those situations! Action is key and I was searching for mine while eighteen keys jingled in my pocket. I just needed to pick one and see if it worked.

It was later that night when Chuck and I met again after dinner to discuss joining the Free Agent Academy faculty as the Roadmap Professor. Now I had an expertise I could share, and a platform from which to do it.

And that's where not only this book began to take shape, but the rest of my life along with it.

I hope this book hits you in the same way Chuck's 2x4 hit me, and allows you to expand your potential and accomplish more than you currently believe is possible.

No Big Deal

Your success will often appear to be "no big deal" to those who meet you only after you find success. They will not see the before, during and after, only the after. They will think you had it easy…a natural talent or a benefactor clearing your path.

Some will know you before and after, but will not know the struggles and efforts you went through to find success. They will be jealous, but some may still be inspired—believing that they may be able to find success if you did.

Only those who walk with you or have walked the path before you will appreciate the work you have done. They will know it wasn't easy. They will know the pain and the struggle, the doubt and the fear. They will understand how many times you almost gave up, and they will know the perseverance it took for you to keep going.

It only looks easy to the outsider. So if you want this thing called success, get ready to work hard. It won't be easy and it isn't guaranteed. But if you dream big and give it your all, it will be worth it.

The Big Deal

Because of its routine nature and his constant practice, a doctor may dismiss his efforts during surgery as no big deal. A patient may do the same, saying he had no other choice but to do what was required, yet it took significant effort not to simply accept his fate but to do something about it. Following through is not as easy as it sounds.

It is at this point that many of us talk ourselves out of our greatness. Don't do that! Give thanks to God for the entirety of what He has given you and then go do great things with it!

It is a BIG DEAL!

The Simple Strategic Plan

The Simple Strategic Plan, or SSP, is a tool developed by Chuck Bowen that he used in his coaching practice.

My first exposure to it was confusing, even though it was just a simple document with nine sections. There was very little formatting and I wasn't quite sure what to do with it. I had a sense that it was something powerful; I just couldn't figure it out.

When I finally heard Chuck do a presentation on it, the lights came on! I saw firsthand how it could be used to funnel high-level, foundational concepts like mission and vision into action steps.

When I became the Roadmap Professor at Free Agent Academy, I reformatted the SSP document to make it more visually appealing. I also added instructions to help others "get it" faster than I did. I started teaching the tool to FAA members, guiding them through it, and reviewing their plans. That effort was the starting point for this book (Part 2 of the book walks through the SSP in detail).

ACTION
STEPS

GOALS

KEY STRATEGIES

SWOT ANALYSIS

BUSINESS OBJECTIVES

VISION NARRATIVE

CORE VALUES

MISSION

SWOT

The Layers of the SSP Pyramid

Some people took to it more quickly than others. Some abandoned it. But I believe everyone who took the course gained new knowledge and awareness of the importance of planning. The SSP is critical to my planning. And even if it isn't fully adopted, it will at least create more focus and intentionality for all who make the effort to use it.

Today the SSP is my primary planning tool. Once I got a solid version of it completed, the quarterly review and updates became much easier to do. I now have a quarterly plan that is broken into weekly mini-plans and tasks. I am focused and getting more done than I ever have before—and I'm working on the most important things first.

This book may take a while to read and digest. It may be a struggle to complete your first SSP and feel confident that it will work. Trust the process. If you stick with it you can have the power and focus to realize your dreams and ideas, and, ultimately, put your potential to work!

How to Read This Book

Planning can be a boring topic, so I worked hard to keep the book flowing and as engaging as possible. Hopefully this is the most exciting book on business planning and strategy you've ever read!

To get the most out of it, I recommend that you read the book from cover to cover (as quickly as you can while still comprehending the concepts). It's a fairly fast read.

Make some notes along the way, but resist the urge to complete each step of your plan in Part 2 until you have an overall perspective of the planning process. This will help you to keep from getting stuck on any single step.

Once you've finished the book, go back through it more slowly, starting at Part 2 to begin planning. Do what you can in each of the nine sections and move to the next one. Go back if new ideas occur. Approach it in a linear fashion, but bounce around to capture all of your thoughts. Move quickly and develop your full plan within two weeks.

Download the Simple Strategic Plan (SSP) template at ConquerYourKryptonite.com (the diagrams in the book are to help comprehension and familiarization...you'll need more space to capture the contents of your plan).

Once your plan is complete, get to work! Use the advice and concepts from Part 3 to guide your efforts. The important thing is to start using a plan to structure your work. You will learn what works and what doesn't as you execute. Read it again as you build your next quarterly plan and continue to use it as a reference for future plans.

Have fun and go do good work!

PART ONE

PREPARING TO PLAN

Before you can build an effective plan, you need to attain proper perspective. Examine exactly what you are trying to do and why. You need to know what motivations are driving you to take on the challenge. If you can't, those motivations won't be there to help you through the difficulties of execution.

In Part One, you'll learn the value of building an effective foundation before you start the planning process, and learn how to drive through either a lack of planning knowledge or previous failures.

Most people are not natural planners. But if you're willing to learn and experiment, you can develop a Simple Strategic Plan that works for you.

Chapter 1
Desire and Paralysis

This chapter outlines the desires people have to start a business, implement an idea or achieve a goal, along with the reasons that so many people look back and see a collection of unexecuted ideas. Their dreams may be dead or dying, all because it seemed too difficult or overwhelming once the need for action (the act of doing) began.

Kryptonite is real and will paralyze you. It will take your powers before you even start if you let it. Don't.

What is Desire?

I believe there's a burning desire buried in the heart of every person. It exists in various forms: ideas, dreams, goals and visions. The motivation may be selfish, altruistic, or somewhere in between.

Desire is the word we give to that thing buried deep within our hearts. You know that thing? It's that persistent longing for something or someone. Nothing can make it go away, and even if we give up on it with our minds, we can still feel the scar of it on our hearts.

There are good desires and bad desires. This isn't a self-help book, so I'm not going to create a manifesto on telling the difference. Just focus on the good desires, the God-given desires, as you work your plans.

Take delight in the Lord, and He will give you the desires of your heart.
– *Psalm 37:4 (NIV)*

The Struggle of Planning

There are some rare individuals who find planning as easy as breathing. They revel in it. Complex plans seem to come as easily to them as mud pies to a four-year-old. But for the rest of humanity, planning is intimidating and stressful.

Stress manifests itself differently for different people. Some become hyper, some become paralyzed. Many times it's because we aren't clear on what we really want...then we feel the pressure to plan just to get something done, and those plans rarely produce results. They are either planned and re-planned without any execution, or sit unfinished (also without any execution).

But successful plans do not necessarily require complexity. While planning comes more naturally to some than others, it can be learned.

Action Required

Planning can be very similar to prayer. You can lift up your heart to God, sharing your desires... often in great detail. But if you simply sit back and wait for God to make it happen, you're missing the point.

God tends to show up once you're on your way. It is the same with planning. You cannot build a plan and expect it just to happen.

You have to do the work! You have to execute! You have to make it happen!

Planning for a business or idea isn't that different from planning a vacation or where to have dinner. Without some kind of plan in place, you are completely reactionary (shiny object syndrome). Without a plan it's easy to move aimlessly from one task to another.

> The key is not to prioritize what's on your schedule, but to schedule your priorities.
> – Stephen Covey, *The Seven Habits of Highly Effective People*

Think it's really as simple as time management? You have to do more than manage your time. You must control your *priorities* and what you do with your time.

Some people naturally think long-term, while others only think in the short-term. But if we are only focused on the long-term, we forget to act today. And if we only think about today, we have no vision for a greater tomorrow. You need to find the middle ground in order to get traction. Better yet, you have to find the place that gets you the results that you desire…that is when you begin to discover your **sweet spot**.

But how do you find it? How do you marry the long-term vision with short-term action? What you need is a planning framework that delivers a funnel to go from the big picture to actionable details. You need a plan that allows you to avoid the paralysis of perfectionism—building a perfect plan that never sees any action.

> All you need is the plan, the road map, and the courage to press on to your destination.
> – Earl Nightingale

What you need is to get your thoughts out of your head and heart and onto paper, and to act boldly to make things happen. A blank sheet of paper is no good…just as an overwhelming plan is no good.

Not every decision is life and death. As my mentor Chuck Bowen says, "The only life and death decisions are…life and death."

Don't over think or over plan. Find the balance…prudent risk taking means that we don't know how everything is going to work out, but we know enough to know that we have a good chance (or that it's our only option for success).

Let's explore some of the biggest hurdles in planning:

Never Planned Before – If you've never made a plan, it's a foreign concept and you don't know what it's supposed to look like. Yet most of us have made plans without knowing it.

Little girls dream of their wedding day for years…it's basic planning in some ways, probably closer than what we do when we dream of being successful in business.

Plan enough to have a few things known in advance, and have a big picture, but just enough to get going and not be stuck. It may seem contradictory, but simple and strategic can go together.

Doing It Alone – Most people who want to start a business or pursue a goal try to do it alone. The concept of creating something alone and revealing it to the world is a lie. You need support, input, and feedback to make things work best. You can use focus groups and test markets, but at a minimum find like-minded and like-hearted people who will support you and give you honest feedback.

Beware if you find yourself so head-down that you never come up for air. The world may change and not need it anymore by the time you release it. (Pity the man who perfected videotape after DVD technology became ubiquitous.)

Finding a community is powerful. Finding a partner is powerful. Don't go it alone. Often what we struggle with becomes the foundation of our greatest success. There's power in the network (more on this in Chapter 16).

BE Before You Can DO – Zig Ziglar is famous for many reasons, including his "Be, Do, Have" philosophy. You have to BE the right kind of person (character, beliefs, etc.) and DO the required work to HAVE the things in life that matter most. Be-Do-Have.

Doing the work connects who you are and the results you'll have. Action glues BE and HAVE together to get BEHAVE! Your behavior (character plus action) dictates what you have.

People struggle with goal setting even though it's incredibly important. Doubt sets in because we don't have clarity on what we're supposed to be. What is our purpose? What is our style or strength or passion? It shakes our foundation when we don't know what God or even other people know about us already.

We want to find a way to escape (maybe a job or financial situation) and we jump into any business opportunity, even if it doesn't fit. The truth is that once we know ourselves, we can find something that fits. Running away can be as bad as the "get rich quick" mentality.

Therefore everyone who hears these words of mine and puts them into practice is like a wise man who built his house on the rock. The rain came down, the streams rose, and the winds blew and beat against that house; yet it did not fall, because it had its foundation on the rock.
– *Matthew 7:24-25 (NIV)*

Begin with a foundation of knowing yourself and behaving in a manner that fits who you are—this will launch you into action better than anything else.

Along the way, be careful not to ignore what you learn about yourself…accept it and use it. Build the plan using other resources or people you need to balance out your business. Maximize your strengths and compensate for your weaknesses—even Superman had Kryptonite to worry about, and you have more weaknesses than he does.

If you hate details, you probably shouldn't be managing inventory or accounting (though someone has to do it). If you love details, go for it (but don't miss the big picture).

Speaking of foundations, make sure that your foundation is solid. Set it firmly on the key areas needed in the business. If you don't, you may find some success at first, but eventually it won't stand anymore. It will crumble and instead of disappearing, it'll be a tattered mess and a constant reminder of your failure. (If that's already happened to you, know that you can clear the wreckage and rebuild bigger and better on a solid foundation.)

It's a Journey, Not a Destination – Planning at its best is an ongoing process. No one can plan for every possible contingency. Plans lay out the roadmap to a destination, but a map won't always show that the bridge you see on paper is out in real life. Eventually you'll need to take a detour in order to reach your destination.

Gardens grow fruits and vegetables...and weeds. There's no avoiding it...to be successful, a gardener must remove the weeds. In the same manner, you will need to adjust your plan along the way.

No plan of operations extends with certainty beyond the first encounter with the enemy's main strength. *[AKA: No plan survives contact with the enemy.]*
– General Helmuth von Moltke,
   On Strategy

If you're seeking to do something more than a static accomplishment, then you need to accept the fact that your destination is probably not tangible. It's not a place you arrive at and stop. It's the place you want to go to and never see the finish line. But there is accomplishment along the path. In fact, this attitude will likely see you accomplish more than you could have imagined when you set out. You'll look back and be amazed!

Dreaming

Dreaming is not the same as planning. A plan is the physical manifestation of your intention. The plan is going to give the dream legs. It gives confidence and boldness.

After laying out your plan, if you still want more information and detail before you can move forward, something probably isn't right at your core. You aren't clear on the dream

People with passion have infinite energy to make it happen, regardless of the information they have. They will have ups and downs like anyone else, but they figure it out along the way.

You can either learn to live with your Kryptonite or you can conquer it. Do what others don't and you will have a distinct strategic advantage.

Don't Be Intimidated by the Plan

Building a plan can be overwhelming—even with a template like the Simple Strategic Plan (SSP) that's only a few pages long. But if you know your core, your journey will be easier.

I needed more than a process and a tool when I started. I also needed a guide like Chuck Bowen who could help me wrap my mind around what all the SSP was trying to do. I needed someone to explain the nuances. Honestly, I needed someone I trusted to walk me through it before I could believe that it works.

And it does.

Optimism and Pessimism

How you think matters. How you act matters more.

Whether you see the glass half full or half empty is not the only indicator of your future success. Some people are full of hope and believe things will always work out for the best. Others see doom and gloom around every corner.

However you see the world, realize that you can be successful if you do the work. Being positive and doing nothing will generate nothing. Being negative and fighting everything that crosses your path can still lead to success.

The truth is that no one is always optimistic or always pessimistic. There are slices of life and in different situations we react differently.

One exercise that helps is to think unrealistically by imagining the best and worst case scenarios.

In a best case, nothing you do can go wrong and everything works out for everyone no matter what. Unrealistic? You bet, but it's good for dreaming and visioning. It gives you something to aim at, and can fuel you to overcome the challenges that arise.

In the worst case, nothing you do matters or makes a difference and everything falls apart. It's also pretty unrealistic, as some things are bound to work out from time to time (even if by accident!). But once you know what rock bottom looks like, it helps you move forward knowing that 1) it isn't likely to be that bad and 2) the worst case is generally survivable!

So aim for realism while being aware of the unrealistic extremes. Do your best to analyze a situation or opportunity or problem and determine the most likely outcomes. Fight through your fears and obstacles and defend against overconfidence.

The Destroyer of Ideas

Remember Medusa, the tragic figure from Greek mythology with snakes for hair? With one look she could turn any living thing to stone.

Too many good ideas die before they even get to battle Medusa. The fear that she may gaze upon them is enough to make someone keep quiet or neglect to fight for their implementation. And while it's true that some ideas and dreams are destroyed in the attempt to give them life, it's also true that some succeed. Let's figure out how not to look back on our lives and see the frozen statues of failed dreams or, worse...those that were never attempted.

We all have dreams. In order to make dreams come into reality, it takes an awful lot of determination, dedication, self-discipline, and effort.
– Jesse Owens

Why We Fail

Understanding why we fail is the first step in learning how to change our behavior and start succeeding. As we examine the reasons we fail, the reasons we succeed are also evident.

1) Procrastination/Fear of Failure

Inaction is stagnation, and stagnation is degradation. There are times when we can decide *not* to decide, but when executing a plan, "waiting" is rarely a valid strategy if something is a top priority. So if we're frozen with indecision, we aren't staying where we are—we're actually moving away from where we want to go!

Procrastination is the constant delaying of activity (when mixed with the planning process, my friend John DiMare calls it "plancrastination"). It's finding distractions or pretending that the work or a bad situation will resolve itself. The world doesn't work like that, so why do we fall into that trap? Break out of it and you can break free to achieve your dreams.

Fearing failure can cause the same kind of paralysis as procrastination. We must act or we will fail. Most people fail every day at all kinds of things. Think of it as trial and error, not failure. Keep trying and keep doing until you find something that works. At least you'll be busy learning, and not sitting on your butt wishing all day (or cowering in fear and living in regret).

Failure has been correctly identified as the line of least persistence.
– Zig Ziglar, *See You at the Top*

2) Lack of Hope or Self-Confidence
The Bible states that "Hope deferred makes the heart sick." (Proverbs 13:12). Why would we perform an activity if there wasn't at least a small hope for success? We wouldn't. But with hope, we can storm the beaches of Normandy to fight tyranny. With hope, we can run into a burning building to save a child. With hope, we can do amazing things. So we have to have hope.

But how do we get hope? I think it comes from both logic and emotion. We can logically assess a situation, no matter how complicated, and find a path that has a positive result, even if it rests upon several unlikely factors turning our way. Unlikely is different from impossible. Unlikely implies possible. But logic alone isn't enough to move us. We have to get our hearts in the game. Maybe it's anger. Maybe it's the potential for joy. When we find it, we can act.

Let's Go!

Logic provides the map. Emotion fuels the engine. Together they take us where we want to go.

Self-confidence is similar in that it's a lack of belief in our ability to do something we want or need to do. We have to find a way to believe. We need to have some success doing something similar first, or we need to gain some new knowledge or experience before we tackle the thing that steals our confidence. Confidence can be grown.

Sometimes we just have to make a leap of faith. We may believe that something won't work, but sometimes, if we try anyway…it does!

3) Don't Know How

We also fail because we don't know how to do something. I have no talent for most mechanical tasks. I've even managed to mess up simple tasks like changing the oil in a car (I pay someone to do it now). But if I wanted to, I could find someone with the knowledge who could teach me (desire to learn is the key). Not knowing how to do something is very different from not having the ability to do something. I can't throw a 100-mph fastball. But I can learn how to throw a strike.

Most of the things that stop us aren't things that we can't do, but the things we refuse to learn. Not knowing is an excuse, and one that can be overcome. So go learn something! (Or, like changing my oil, hire it out and move on to bigger priorities.)

4) Not Written Down

There is a strange power in having something written down. I'm not saying it's mystical, just that when we write something down instead of only thinking about it, it becomes real. Words on paper stare back at you. They challenge you. They encourage you. And you are much more likely to work to make them happen.

One of the most amazing stories about this power comes from my friend Alan Jackson (no, not the country singer). This Alan Jackson is from Paducah, Kentucky. He had attended a seminar where everyone was encouraged to write down 50 things that they wanted to accomplish in their lives. It wasn't really a bucket list, just a list of 50 things. While doing the assignment, he quickly wrote down 49 items but then got stuck. Someone else in the seminar wrote that he wanted to learn how to fly an airplane, so Alan put that down, too. After all, he needed 50 items, and that sounded as good as anything else.

After the seminar, that list, along with the rest of the conference materials, went into a box. It was hidden away until Alan found it several years later while packing for a move. He dropped the box and out popped the list.

Remembering the assignment inside, he started going through the list to see how well he had done. To his amazement, Alan found that he had accomplished every goal on the list except one…learning how to fly!

Here was a list that he hadn't even looked at, yet every goal was completed except for the one. How is that possible? It's the power of writing them down! (I highly recommend reviewing them from time to time anyway!)

Reduce your plan to writing. The moment you complete this, you will have definitely given concrete form to the intangible desire.
    – Napoleon Hill, *Think and Grow Rich*

5) No Personal Ownership

So what happened to Alan's goal of learning to fly? Why did he accomplish every goal on his list except for that one? He certainly had the ability and the resources. (It's not a cheap thing, but taking flying lessons isn't out of reach if you budget for it.)

The reason Alan didn't learn how to fly is because Alan

didn't want to learn how to fly. It wasn't really his goal; it was someone else's. His heart was never set on flying, so writing it down didn't make any difference.

You have to have personal ownership of your goals. If it's a goal worth attaining, and one that will take considerable work, effort and sacrifice, it has to be something you want to do. So own your goals. Pursue the things you want to do. No one climbs a mountain just because it's there...they climb it because they want to climb it. They want to own it.

He who would accomplish little must sacrifice little; he who would achieve much must sacrifice much; he who would attain highly must sacrifice greatly.
– James Allen, *As a Man Thinketh*

6) Not Specific and Measurable

Zig Ziglar says that if you aim at nothing you'll hit it every time. Put another way, how can you know you've arrived at your destination if you didn't know where you were going in the first place?

Losing weight is the classic example. Simply saying you want to lose weight isn't enough. You have to state how much. Ten pounds? Twenty? One hundred? Until you know how much, you can't know how well you're doing. If you lose one pound, you've lost weight...but did you realize the change in your life that you wanted? Probably not.

Document a number AND define the change you desire so you know when you get there. Make your goals specific and measurable. Otherwise they get lost in the fog of improvement.

7) No Deadlines or Accountability

The other side of being specific and measurable is the deadline. Losing ten pounds is a great goal, but if it takes you 30 years, did it really impact your life that much?

Having deadlines helps to hold you accountable. It helps you to say **"yes"** to the things that are hard and move you forward, and **"no"** to the things that are easy (lazy) and move you backward.

Share your goal with others so they can remind you and hold you accountable. Accountability isn't always fun, but it can be the difference between achievement and failure.

Every day, even your days off, you are either moving towards or away from your dream.
– Catalyst John

Understanding the Journey Ahead

If your dream or goal or wish or idea is big, then your journey will have to be big, too. This isn't about mapping out a strategy for getting milk and bread from the grocery store five miles from your home. This is more like Frodo carrying a ring of power to Mt. Doom. There will be obstacles. There will be a sense of impending failure. This will not be easy. But if you're committed to seeing it through, it will be worth it!

One January, I celebrated my birthday at a Free Agent Academy event in Woodland Park, Colorado. My friend Kevin Miller started FAA, and he and his wife Teri got me a little present. It's a simple ceramic wall hanging that states: "*Success is not a destination, but a journey.*"

It reminds me that although it may be hard, I need to enjoy the everyday moments of the journey and not just the fleeting moment of success to come in the future. That moment will come and go, but the journey and the lives I touch (and am touched by) along the way are much more important.

Don't Be An Action Figure... Be Action!

Action is the only thing that makes ideas happen. Not dreaming or wishing. Not talking or contemplating. Action!

Generally I'm not a proponent of doing something just to do it. I'm more the natural planning type. But I can also easily fall into the trap of analysis paralysis—the process by which planning overtakes any and all action, leading to the death and destruction of an idea or project. Too much planning will kill ideas, just as not having a plan will.

If you're reading this book, you probably want to start a business, improve a business, implement an idea or achieve a big goal. Noble and just causes, all!

The trick is that our pursuits to achieve lofty goals quickly become bogged down by reality. Sure, it's great to sit back and dream about owning a business, driving a nice car, and experiencing all the perks that come with being the boss. It's fun to think about how your brilliant idea will improve the world or save lives. But at some point you have to move out of the dreaming phase and into the doing. Again, action makes things happen.

> We cannot totally control the future, but we can accomplish some pretty amazing things if we plan, focus, and act on them.
> – Deb Ingino

When we get to the work of making it happen, we soon realize what hard work it is. And hard work isn't always fun. Passion will take you a long way, but you're going to need more than passion. You're going to need a plan.

Strategy is Hard

Most people don't like to plan. Planning is hard, and strategy is harder. For most, strategy means knowing every possible move from beginning to end. They think of chess masters staring at the board as they watch their opponents. From memory they utter strangely-named strategies to protect the King and slay the enemy!

The truth is that strategy is nothing more than thinking more than one step ahead at a time. If you can think a few steps ahead, great. That will help you. But one step ahead is the beginning of strategic thinking and strategic planning.

We fall into the trap of believing we have to know every possible path and every possible outcome. The truth is that there are probably an infinite number of outcomes and paths to those outcomes. Don't let that discourage you...let it encourage you! If there are really that many paths, then there's probably more than one that can take you to your destination.

Moving forward means that you instantly begin eliminating possible paths. Looking forward means you are strategic about the paths that lie ahead, and can attempt to pick the best one.

Why Plan in the First Place?

Zig Ziglar once told a story about a man getting braces on his teeth. When asked why he would do such a thing, he replied that it's not about getting braces...it's about the smile.

A plan should not exist for itself...there has to be a result! That result is why you plan in the first place.

Chapter 2:
The Mythical Business Plan

You don't need a business plan, you need a plan for your business. Traditional business plans have their place when going to a banker for a loan or an investor for startup cash, or when working with the Small Business Administration. But once the funding is secured, the plans gather dust. Instead, let's do the work to create an actionable and realistic plan that speaks specifically to the idea and the owner(s) of the idea. Let's build something that works.

Kryptonite cannot be eliminated, but it can be contained. Are you willing to do what it takes to succeed in spite of it?

What is the Purpose of Your Plan?

No one builds a plan without putting some thought into the purpose of the plan. By definition, you cannot build a plan unless you have a purpose in mind. It doesn't have to be fancy, but it has to have some kind of goal, something to be achieved or constructed or accomplished. That is your target.

So if you want to start a business, you need to build a business plan, right?

The Small Business Administration and your local bank may hate me for saying it, but odds are you don't need a business plan. Traditional business plans are designed to get you a loan. While some components of them may be useful in the process of mapping out your business, most of these plans gather dust as soon as the loans are approved.

Let's take a different approach.

A Plan for Your Business

You don't need a business plan. You need a plan for your business.

First, you need to know what it is you are trying to accomplish. What are your motivations? Why do you want to do what you want to do?

Don't dismiss those questions too quickly. They are of vital importance (note: vital means essential to life...we throw the word around in our culture too much—this really is vital to the life of your business!).

Why is this important? Because it's hard to start, grow, and run a business. Accomplishing a meaningful goal is hard. Living a dream doesn't happen automatically.

There will be obstacles. If you're going to find a way around, over, under or through those obstacles, you're going to need perseverance. Perseverance doesn't come from a financial reward. It comes from passion.

The Power of Passion

Passion is a burning desire, a fundamental belief in something—a belief so powerful that no objection will deter you.

Without passion for your idea, the idea will die. It lives and breathes only because you feed it with passion. Your passion drives you to action. Your passion drives you to overcome all obstacles and objections. When no one else in the world believes in you or your idea, passion—for better or worse—will fuel your efforts.

Passion and Failure

I dated two girls before getting married (and I married the first one!). I only ever asked out a handful of girls because I was too scared of rejection to try. More than 20 years later, I realize how silly this was.

So what if she said no? There were a lot of other girls out there.

Today I have to remind myself that the same rules apply to pursuing my passions. I can try and I may fail, or I can **NOT** try and definitely fail.

Real vs. Fake Obstacles

Fear is a powerful thing. It, like Medusa, can paralyze. Fear can also move us to action.

Crossing a busy street during rush hour can be scary. But if you see a child in the middle of the road and you're called into action, fear melts away. After it's over, you don't even know why or how you did what you did.

A friend and client of mine recently had back surgery after years of pain and suffering. The surgery offered hope that he could return to a normal life. But there's nothing normal about his life anymore.

While touring a beach along the Gulf Coast to see the impact of the 2010 BP oil spill, he and his wife came upon a devastating sight. A small group of people had gathered and they were pulling something from the water. When he realized it was a person's body, he told his wife to run to help them because she's a nurse.

Meanwhile, he's running behind her as fast as he can, just five weeks after surgery. Not a good thing. Then he heard a cry for help from others on the beach. There was someone else in the water.

Once he realized what was happening, he didn't think. He sprinted. He dove into the water. He was on a mission fueled by passion. And it almost cost him his life.

Running was bad enough, but the waves bent his already tender back. Exhausted and having failed to reach the person in the water, he collapsed on the beach.

This was a tragic event that could have been avoided. No one should have been in the water that day. The oil was bad and the waves were worse. Sadly, two people died.

Looking back on the event, my friend said he didn't know why he did what he did. He wasn't thinking. It was foolish to attempt it so soon after surgery.

But nothing could have stopped him, either. His heart and his love for people wouldn't allow him to stand on the beach and not try. He's still suffering from that day, both physically and emotionally. But he'd be in worse shape if the only images flashing through his mind represented his view from the beach.

Passion will drive you and give you the power to attempt the unlikely and impossible. It may end in failure, but wouldn't you rather do your best than live with the regret of never trying?

The most powerful weapon on earth is the human soul on fire.

– Field Marshal Ferdinand Foch

Asking for Help

It is arrogant to ask for help if you don't have some idea of what you need help with. Building a basic plan of action will facilitate the conversation and make it more effective. Be thoughtful enough about your own business to write it down, and you'll get more and better help.

If you share your SSP with another person, they will gain an instant understanding of who you are, what you're doing and where you're going. That understanding can help them help you.

Read more on not going it alone in Chapter 16.

Chapter 3:
Simple IS Powerful

Taking an idea out of the head and heart and making it happen is hard. Planning seems overwhelming because there are a million little things to do. Each new task spawns two or three more, and soon an infinite number of actions drown out all of the fun, excitement and realism from an otherwise great idea. But complex plans aren't needed for most small businesses and startups. Simple plans can yield incredible results.

Strength is more than brute force. Superman is strong *AND* smart. A simple strategy will defeat a complex one almost every time. It sees action sooner.

Breakdown to Breakthrough

It's important to have big dreams and big goals. Some people thrive in the world of BIG and can make things happen with ease. But BIG can paralyze many people. And there are plenty of clichés out there to make it easier:

- How do you eat an elephant? One bite at a time!
- The journey of a thousand miles begins with the first step.

Even I get tired of hearing these old sayings, but the fact is there's some powerful truth in them. My mouth simply isn't big enough to swallow an elephant whole (even a baby one!). But if I eat it one bite at a time, over the course of weeks or months, I could in fact eat the whole thing (I think I'll skip the bones).

The point is that taking a very large task and trying to do it all at once is normally impossible. If it's going to take significant effort, it's going to take time. And the best way to take that big goal and make it manageable is to break it down into step-by-step (or bite-by-bite) actions.

Let's look at some significant examples:

Weight Loss – Imagine you need to lose 100 pounds. That's a heavy task (sorry, couldn't resist!). What would be a realistic and healthy timeframe to lose 100 pounds? A year? That would be less than two pounds per week. It's aggressive, but probably realistic. If your mindset is on losing just two pounds, that seems a lot easier than 100 pounds. The 100-pound goal is still there, and is something to strive for, but the actions you take on a daily basis are focused on how to lose just two pounds. And after a few weeks at two pounds each, you'll see that you've lost five, then ten, then 20 pounds. Progress builds momentum!

Becoming Debt Free – Dave Ramsey is one of my heroes. I've taught Financial Peace University more than 15 times and that experience put me on the path I'm on today. He's helped thousands and perhaps millions of people get on a better path with their money. His Baby Steps offer a strategic, step-by-step approach to getting out of debt and building wealth.

One of the major tenets of his plan is to pay off all of your debts except the house in order from smallest to largest. Two key things in that approach: 1) He wants you to have a quick win by paying off the smallest debt (just like the first week of weight loss) and 2) He delays the BIG debt, a mortgage, until long after the other debts are paid in full.

Does he want you to pay off the house? Yes. Do you? Absolutely! But if you put all your focus and energy in the BIG one, you'll get taken down by the little ones long before you get there.

Difficulties are just things to overcome, after all.

– Sir Ernest Henry Shackleton, *The Heart of the Antarctic*

Climbing Mt. Everest – Standing majestically over the Himalayas is the tallest mountain in the world. Climbing Everest is a daunting task, with a success rate of about 29% and about 2% of climbers dying in the process![2] It's a serious undertaking. So why would anyone want to do it?

Part of the attraction is the difficulty. But I don't think anyone would be wise to put climbing Mt. Everest as the first mountain on their to-do list. They start with some smaller mountains. They learn and grow and get stronger. Every small step up the practice mountains is the same size as every step up the biggest mountain.

Another thing about climbing a mountain like Everest is

---

[2] http://www.adventurestats.com/tables/EverestAgeFat.shtml

that you don't do it all at once. You have to pace yourself and do it in stages. Along the way are base camps. These base camps allow you to acclimate, refresh, recover, and prepare for the next leg of the journey. They are milestones to accomplish and look forward to. Without them, no one could climb the mountain.

So in order to have the big breakthrough and accomplish BIG goals, it's important to break them into smaller pieces first. Every project has a halfway point, and there's a halfway point to that halfway point, and so on. It can be done one step at a time!

Zeno's Paradox

Zeno of Elea (great name!) was a Greek philosopher from the 5th century B.C. He is famous for creating philosophical paradoxes documented by Aristotle.

I first heard one of them in an algebra class in high school, and it's stuck with me ever since. It basically goes like this:

Suppose I wish to shoot an arrow at a target ten feet away. In order for the arrow to hit the target, it must first travel halfway, or five feet. But in order to travel the five feet to halfway, it must travel half of that distance, or two-and-a-half feet. It must always travel half of the distance first, dividing in half to infinity. Therefore, the arrow can never reach the destination.

Of course, we all know that an arrow *can* travel the ten feet and hit the target. That's what makes it a paradox. It can both hit and not hit the target based on logic and observation.

(The answer lies in Calculus, a subject I never mastered. Basically it has to do with dividing an infinite distance with an infinite time to get a finite result or something. Try Google if you want a better explanation!)

What I love about this paradox is not the paradox itself, but the concept of breaking any task into smaller tasks. If I have a major goal, I can move myself halfway to that goal. And before I can get halfway to that point, I can go halfway still. Eventually I get down not to infinitesimally small steps, but realistic and doable steps.

The division of the steps may be different for different people, depending on our skills, talents and abilities. But at some point, we look and say that the first step of our journey, no matter how small, is doable! Therefore, the big goal, no matter how big, is also doable if we will only take each step on the path to achieving it.

Bottom Line: Do What Works!

Do a quick search on the internet for project management tools and methodologies and you'll find hundreds if not thousands of ways to get things done. Which one is right? I can't tell you.

That's because there isn't just one that works. Many work, and some will work better for you than others do. If you're using a spreadsheet to track your finances instead of Quickbooks, you're not wrong. You might find Quickbooks is better, or you might not. What you have to evaluate is if what you're doing is getting the results you need, or if you can do it better.

Never become married to a tool or process and shut out all possibility of trying something else. But at the same time, if what's working for you is working, don't jump into something new too quickly.

In this book I'm going to outline a planning methodology called the Simple Strategic Plan (SSP). It's a great tool and it really can make you think about things that are typically overlooked when planning. I believe the SSP can help most people do more and achieve more than they've done and achieved before. But will everyone like it better than what they're doing today? No. Will everyone do it the way I lay it out? No. In fact, I'm guessing most people will adjust it to fit their personal preferences.

Some people will type it out on their computers. Others need to write it down in their own handwriting. One way is not better than the other.

However, there are critical aspects of the methodology that cannot be skipped. The method of doing the steps may vary, but the value of each of the steps is clear and evident.

Evaluate all of your tools and processes to see if they are working or if they can be better. And if you or your team ever catch yourself saying, "but that's the way we've always done it" when questioned, then it's time to evaluate what you're doing. It may be the best way...but don't let it be there without intentionally deciding it's the best way. Always strive to find a better answer.

Origins of the Simple Strategic Plan (SSP)

Chuck Bowen was a successful business planner in his corporate jobs, rising the ladder to become a CEO. He worked with start-up companies for about six years where he had to do strategic plans in order to get funding, go public, or complete mergers.

After doing a lot of them, he began laughing at the silliness of it all. Once the planning was done, what was left that would actually be used to do the work? He realized that the key to success relied more heavily on what happens AFTER you get the funding and have to do the work.

When he left the corporate world to start his own coaching business, he realized that it helps to think through (out loud and written down) what someone wants their business to be. Most clients seemed to be anti-planning—they weren't thinking forward, strategizing, or even being thoughtful about what they wanted.

And no wonder. Too many planning templates and examples are too long (multiple pages of contents and hundreds of pages long). Military war plans may need to sit in binders on shelves for every possible contingency, but that's not what is needed for small businesses.

Most people are not natural planners. A tool was needed, and Chuck combined several things to come up with the SSP. It includes the things a business needs but it's set up in a way that small business owners can understand...so they can act when it's time to act.

Effective vs. Efficient

Are you doing things right, or are you doing the right things? Ponder that for a moment.

I'm a perfectionist. I like to do things right. No typos. No crumbs. No mess. Perfect is always my goal and my motivation. But that attitude can keep me from accomplishing anything!

When it comes to my work, nothing is ever really good enough for me. I know that if I read this book after it's published, I will find typos. At that moment, I'll feel a very real emotional failure. (Fact: During the editing process, I found that I had written "Nothing is *every* good enough for me." Glad I found that one before printing!).

I have to learn to get over it and be happy that my book— typos and all—is printed, bound and in my hand. That is the key to being effective.

The words on my screen serve no one and help no one if they cannot be seen. I can scrub out the typos and formatting issues and passive sentences all I want...but I have to finish. I have to get it to an acceptable level of completion and then put it out there. If I don't...you'll never read this. You'll never love it or hate it. And maybe you'll never change your life for the better and pursue your dream—a dream that could change the world and affect billions of lives for thousands of years.

Something flawed and shipped will trump something beautiful but unshipped every time. Do what Seth Godin tells us to do: Ship It!

Flexibility is Key

When I was training to become an officer in the US Air Force, we were taught a lot about flying (though most of us would never be pilots or even ride in a plane as a regular part of our duties). It was still important for us to understand the basic principles of air combat. And the mantra that was repeated more often than any other: "Flexibility is the key to air power."

I've come to learn since then that flexibility is the key to most strategies and plans. There are always unexpected, unplanned and unforeseen variables once you move from planning to execution. It's important to stay flexible and be able to respond to these emerging factors.

I used to believe that the best way to build something was to make it as strong and rigid as possible. Later I learned how buildings and cars and even wings on airplanes are designed to bend and flex under pressure. They seem solid up close, but they are in constant motion. That flexibility is the source of their strength. They can respond appropriately to external forces.

That which we persist in doing becomes easier to do, not that the nature of the thing itself is changed, but that our power to do is increased.
– Ralph Waldo Emerson

Momentum is Powerful

Nothing helps us tackle a big challenge like having success in a previous challenge. Success begets success.

An object (or objective) in a state of rest has no momentum. That rock sitting there—nothing. That idea or dream in your head and on your heart—nothing. **First you have to get OUT of the state of rest and into the state of ACTION.**

The good news is that any movement toward the objective is the beginning of momentum. It takes commitment. It takes motivation. It takes practice and entering into the unknown.

But momentum exists. Tap into it and learn how to recognize it. Grow it and cultivate it. If you lose it, know how to find it again (if you had it once, you can get it back).

Just make sure it isn't working against you. Momentum works both ways, and will keep you down if you let it. Don't.

PART TWO

BUILDING THE PLAN

It's time to build your plan!

The Simple Strategic Plan is made up of nine steps over the nine chapters in Part Two of the book. Each step builds on the next, but also points back to the others. The first steps build the foundation for the later steps. All of the steps are connected and they support each other.

You may want to take notes as you read through Part Two for the first time, but resist the urge to knock out your plan before finishing the book. Read it all first, then come back and walk through each step after you have a complete view of the process.

Work through each chapter in order. As you discover new things about yourself and your business, go back to the previous step to add relevant details. It's a linear process, but fluid once each step is completed.

Some steps will be easier than others. Keep moving through the process and don't get stuck! Clarity in the difficult steps will come as the plan begins to take shape.

Chapter 4:
Know Thyself (SWOT)

Who are you to think you can make your idea work? You need to believe in yourself and your idea, and the best place to start is to understand yourself. What are your Strengths and Weaknesses? Assess yourself honestly and identify the things you can leverage to make gains, and reinforce yourself against the things that are choking your progress. What are your Opportunities and Threats? Investigate what it is that can take you to the next level or knock you down... act on the former, block the latter.

Kryptonite is only one weakness for our flying friend. If he doesn't have the proper perspective—*knowing the difference between good and evil, right and wrong—*he cannot be a hero.

Who Do You Think You Are?

You need to believe in yourself and your idea if the both of you will be successful. Define your core. Everything else is built upon it.

The first part of building your plan is analyzing who you are and what you bring to the table. You're not perfect, but you are brilliant! You have Strengths and Weaknesses, and how you apply them to your environment and circumstances will dictate your Opportunities and the Threats to your dream.

Understanding Perspective

Gaining proper perspective is the best way to start planning any venture, and it will serve you well if you use it to correct your course along the way of any project.

So what exactly is perspective? Perspective is how you see the world around you. That perspective may be truthful, or it may be biased. Biases are deceiving and we often don't even know they exist.

Pause and question your reality from time to time. Ask yourself if you have a monopoly on right and wrong in any given situation. You may be right. You probably are. But what if you're not? Seek the truth, even when it's difficult to accept.

Proper perspective is foundational for any strategy. Be intentional and use it wisely.

The Importance of (Self) Honesty

The most solid foundation you can build on is the truth. And the easiest person to lie to is YOURSELF.

If your dream is something worth doing, it's going to take a lot of work. It's not likely you're going to stumble into it and find instant success. It's going to be hard.

If you cut corners in your planning process, you'll miss critical pieces—pieces that can destroy your efforts and tempt you to quit.

Even the most robust planning processes miss critical elements that force delays and rework. Quality planning at the beginning can make the journey smoother and allow your initial efforts to take you further before rework begins.

So unless your goal is to build a leaning tower, pour a solid foundation before you begin.

Discover Yourself

The StrengthsFinder evaluation in the *StrengthsFinder 2.0* book by Tom Rath is a great tool. It will help you to identify your top five Strength (talent) areas, and will provide practical application advice to grow your Strengths to maturity.

Other self-evaluation tools like the DISC or Meyers-Briggs profiles can help you capture material for your SWOT.

Just remember that no profile can fully encompass the complexities of who you are as a unique human being. Look it over and pull out the terms and phrases that ring truest.

SWOT

No, this is not about a 1975 TV show (or the 2003 movie remake). However, I wouldn't be surprised to find that a real SWAT team uses a SWOT analysis!

SWOT stands for Strengths, Weaknesses, Opportunities and Threats. Analyzing where you and your team stand is a critical starting place and helps you direct the entirety of the planning process that will unfold in the following chapters.

As you document the SWOT matrix, I recommend that you use detailed bullet points. Don't write a novel, but describe how something applies so that it's defined by a bit more than a single word. And don't go overboard with entries in each category…5-10 should give you a good starting place. You can come back later and add more or adjust as needed.

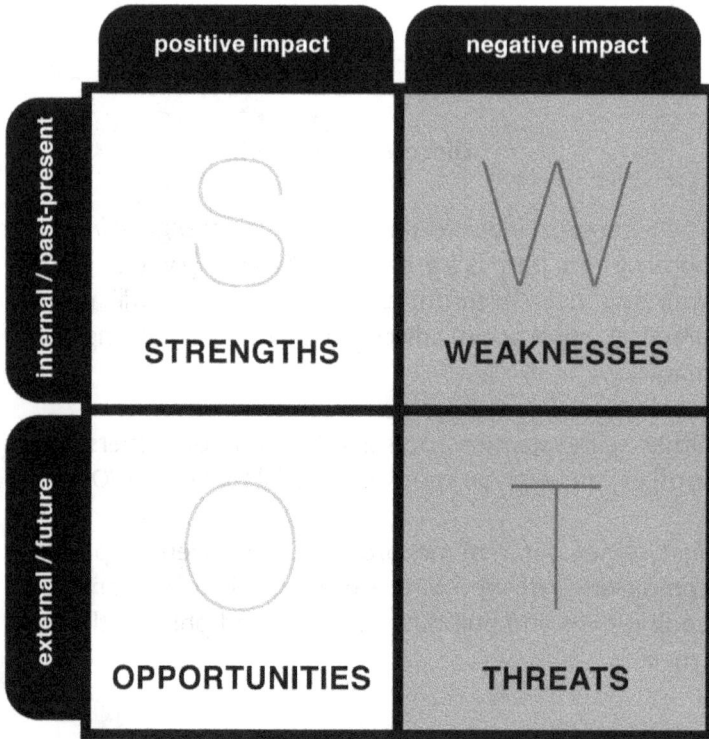

	positive impact	negative impact
internal / past-present	STRENGTHS	WEAKNESSES
external / future	OPPORTUNITIES	THREATS

Let's look at each component of the SWOT analysis:

Strengths – Strengths are what you do inherently well and where you are extraordinary. These are things that work in your favor; things you can leverage to your advantage over and over. They come easily to you and are very powerful and effective. Answer the question: What is going well?

Be Remarkable

Seth Godin talks about being remarkable in his book, *Purple Cow*.

The idea is that if you're driving down a country road and see a bunch of cows, it's not a big deal (unless maybe you live in the big city and never see them).

But what if you saw a purple cow?

My bet is that you'll talk about it (make a remark). And these days you'll also take a picture and post it on Facebook, Instagram, Twitter or whatever other social tools you use.

Seek to be remarkable… that when noticed, people will say something and tell others because it's worth mentioning (just don't cross the line into mere stunts or gimmicks— add value through what you do that is remarkable).

When documenting your Strengths, use bullet points. Look to your experiences: where do you perform well and enjoy yourself most? The intersection of what you do well and what brings value to other people can highlight overlooked Strengths. And in some cases, relationships or connections with other people or organizations can be key Strengths (such as a supportive spouse or incredibly gifted mentor in your corner).

Remember that you don't have to be the best in the world to have a Strength. Often Strengths are untapped areas of potential. Document these Strengths, even if they still need to be developed.

Weaknesses – Now we look at the other side of the coin. If you're a pessimist, this will be easier than defining Strengths.

These are areas that you need to reinforce and defend against. Answer the question: What's not working?

Everyone has Weaknesses (anyone who says they don't is lying). On my SWOT, I list perfectionism as both a Strength and a Weakness. My attention to detail gives me the ability to perform and produce with high levels of excellence. However, if I take this strength too far, it can become a Weakness by leading to paralysis and procrastination.

What do you need to get over? The key here is to be true and honest. Don't put a pretty picture on things, lay it out...the ugly things have to be worked through.

What are you not good at? What things are better left to someone else because you just don't have the talent required to do an adequate job?

Opportunities – Now we begin to look forward. What's going to take us to the next level? What helps us launch or boost our production/profits? You can go back and prioritize them later, but for your first attempt just do a brain dump and get them written down.

This is where you capture your passions, the things that will pull you forward emotionally in your business. If you can't get excited about it, you may be going down the wrong path. This is the time to dream. Explore what exists on the edges of realistic and possible. If you were to share these with other people, they may have varying opinions, but that can be good feedback...especially in terms of finding a market willing to buy.

The key in listing your Opportunities is to document what is going well and what can give you a turbo boost going forward.

Threats – These are the things that may take you down. Think of your competition and how your Weaknesses may affect your actions and reactions.

Threats are the things that can hurt you. If you're already

hurting, it may be better categorized as a Weakness. Threats are generally future oriented, but mentally and emotionally present.

How do we overcome them? Threats are inevitable. They always exist, even if they are strictly internal (i.e. confidence). At this point acknowledge them. You don't want them hiding in a dark corner! Bring them out into the light and they aren't as scary. We'll analyze them later in order to minimize their negative impact.

Optimists and Pessimists

Optimists will have a much easier time documenting Strengths and Opportunities, while pessimists will find Weaknesses and Threats easier.

Remember that you're searching for the truth (proper perspective) and if you put too much effort or content in one area, you'll be out of balance as you continue to plan.

True champions know themselves honestly and build a strategy that accentuates the positive and compensates for the negative.

Navigating the SWOT

When first approaching your SWOT, it can be confusing. It's not always easy to know in which quadrant to place something.

First, don't worry about it. Capturing a truthful observation about yourself or your organization is more important than putting it in the right category. So if you have what I would define as a Threat in your Weaknesses…who cares! It's documented and you still can act on it.

Another thing that can help document your SWOT is to consider whether an item is internal or external. In general, Strengths and Weaknesses will be internal, while Opportunities and Threats will be external. Similarly, Strengths and Weaknesses tend to have a past/present orientation, where Opportunities and Threats are present/future oriented.

Even with all of this it's easy to be confused during your first attempt. Don't worry about it. The categories are likely to bleed into each other...let them bleed here so you can bleed less later.

SWOT Can Be Bigger Than You

Can SWOT work for teams, too? Absolutely!

We carry around the same blind spots/sacred cows for years. SWOT begins to clarify where the organization or team is strong and helps you leverage what it does best (and find additional areas of Opportunity). Also, as Weaknesses and Threats become evident, so do the people you need to get involved or the ones to avoid/remove from your team.

SWOT can help you find ways to expand your reach. It allows you to go to the core of what you do well, and then get help for the rough spots and find the experts to help you through them.

SWOT is a great tool for gaining perspective that can be used for an entire businesses or organization, departments or teams, and even for individual projects.

SSP Instructions:
SWOT

Building a SWOT chart is the first step in building your plan of action. Be honest in assessing each area. The rest of your strategic plan is built upon this exercise. Use simple bullet points.

- **Strengths** – Document what you do inherently well (where are you remarkable?) and other factors that are working in your favor at this point in time. These are the good things that you can leverage to your advantage.

- **Weaknesses** – Enter the things you don't/can't do well right now. These are areas you need to develop into minimum competence or eliminate altogether as you move forward. They are present pains and hurting your efforts.

- **Opportunities** – Write down the things that can take you to the next level once you get going. What can you tap into to get to the next level? You will need to prioritize your activities to take advantage of these areas.

- **Threats** – List the things that are in your way or can take you down (this may include your perceived or real competitors). Counter/eliminate them while moving forward.

SSP Step 1:
SWOT

Strengths:	
1	
2	
3	
4	
5	
6	
7	
8	
9	
10	

Weaknesses:	
1	
2	
3	
4	
5	
6	
7	
8	
9	
10	

Opportunities:	
1	
2	
3	
4	
5	
6	
7	
8	
9	
10	

Threats:	
1	
2	
3	
4	
5	
6	
7	
8	
9	
10	

Download the SSP Template at ConquerYourKryptonite.com.

SSP Evaluation Questions:
SWOT

☐ **Am I being honest with myself?**

Remember we must gain proper perspective. Don't dismiss your Strengths (brag a bit, it's okay!) and don't gloss over painful Weaknesses (we all have them).

☐ **Have you only documented resume fodder?**

This isn't about getting a job. You're working for yourself. Dig deeper and find real abilities, not accolades and honors, achievements and failures—unless they are used to highlight your point.

☐ **What did you miss?**

Ask your spouse, your parents, your friends, your co-workers to review it... anyone that will give you honest answers (responses may vary based on their perspectives).

☐ **Does each entry contain more than a word or two?**

It needs to! What it means to you today may not be as clear months or years from now. For example, if you wrote "Details" as a Weakness, is it because you're too detailed or not enough? Don't write a paragraph, but give it some meat for clarity and completeness.

☐ **Is it balanced?**

It shouldn't be all positive or all negative. We're seeking the truth, not a pep talk or a beat down.

☐ **Does it address all the key areas of life and business?**

Mental, physical, spiritual, emotional, financial, relational, etc.

Chapter 5:
Mission Statement

What do you want to be paid to do?

There is a place in this world for corporate mission statements. There's also a special level of hell for most of them. If the organization doesn't buy into the mission statement, then no amount wordsmithing or gold-plating will make it stick. In a small business, especially in a solo business, a real understanding and articulation of the mission at best means the difference between surviving and thriving, and at worst, whether your business will continue to exist at all.

Without a mission, Superman exists for no reason. His powers are either wasted and unused, or misused as he becomes a bully... or perhaps even a villain.

Priming the Pump

Mission Statements can be hard to write. If you already have an idea of what your business is about, use the following sections to refine your concept and test your resolve for your existing mission. You'll end up with a tighter and more meaningful Mission Statement than what you currently have, or at least have greater resolve to make it happen.

If you're new to the process of documenting a Mission Statement or don't really know what your core business is yet, the following sections will help you move forward.

You'll need a strong sense of what your mission is in order to move forward in the planning process (you can't plan effectively for an unknown target). However, the wording of your Mission Statement is not as important as the passion around your mission at this point in the process. It can and likely will be refined over time…if you nail down the core of it properly from the beginning.

Passion vs. Payment

Doing what you love to do is often payment enough…until the mortgage is due or the kids want to eat.

Too many people leave the dreams of their youth and supplant those passions with a J-O-B. Jobs pay the bills and feed the kids…but too often suck the soul out of people who wanted more out of life.

So how can we reconcile this seeming incompatibility between passion and payment? There are many great resources out there, including books like Dan Miller's *48 Days to the Work You Love* and online communities like his son Kevin Miller's school for self-employment, FreeAgentAcademy.com. But in the end it's as simple as finding the intersection between what you want to do and what someone is willing to pay you for.

Finding the Intersection of Passion and Payment

Here's a simple example of what you can do to start this process: Make a list of all of the things you love to do. Be creative and don't think about jobs or money or anything else...just a list of things you love. It could be drinking coffee, reading books, sports, quilt-making, building birdhouses...anything!

Got it? Now analyze it for ways to get paid to do those things. But don't dismiss them without being creative.

Perhaps you love coffee. You could open a Starbucks franchise, or maybe even start a local coffee house to compete with the big guys. You'll be working non-stop (fueled by caffeine!) and rarely get to leave your town because you have to stay on top of the business.

If that works for you, go for it. But what if you also love to travel? Being stuck in town making coffee all day long is going to conflict with your passion for travel. I smell burnout, not lattés.

There is another option (in fact, there are tons of options). Let's combine both coffee and travel. You could travel the country, blogging and writing reviews of different local coffee houses. You could travel the world, touring coffee fields and buying beans for the coffee shops or big companies. You could take people with you...and create vacations for coffee fanatics to see the bean production and taste coffee all over the world.

See how that works? By knowing what you love (and combinations that fit), you can find a way to make it pay. It may take some work, but if you let passion fuel you and apply some creative thinking, you'll find an intersection between what you love and what you can get paid for.

Do You Give Up or Find the Right Angle?

Several years ago my friend Brett Traudt had a great product he was passionate about: his handmade soap made with natural ingredients. He loves everything about it and finds the process both refreshing and rewarding. The samples I tried were great. So he started to turn it into a business...until he calculated just how much soap he'd have to make to make a living.

Between the challenge of making that much soap and coming up with a successful branding/marketing strategy, the effort just didn't make it worthwhile as a business. That's a good thing to know before you quit your job and invest tens of thousands of dollars in equipment and supplies.

But Brett's story has an interesting twist. He didn't stop making soap. He did it because he enjoyed it and he even sold some. Fast forward a few years and he found his voice through the soap. He combined it with his passion for the outdoors and branded it Mountain Man Soap.

He recently told me, "It took years but Mountain Man Soap came out of who I am. Someone who loves the outdoors and someone who is an expert at soap making. I don't just sell soap... I sell the benefit of the outdoors for your emotional, physical, and spiritual well-being."

If you'd like to get some of Brett's incredible soap, visit MountainManSoap.com.

What Do YOU Want to Be Paid to Do?

Your Mission Statement should further tap into your passion and dreams. It needs to be succinct and clear. It should be structured to be unchanging...a part of your deepest core. But that's not always easy to know when you're starting out. If you find out along the way that it doesn't feel quite right, make changes. Always work to refine it, but operate as if it's an absolute.

Ask yourself: "What's in it for me? What do I want?" Those

questions have to be answered in order for your work to be fully yours and for it to be enjoyable. Your heart has to be present for it to be yours.

This is the intersection of what you love to do and what people are willing to pay you to do. One or the other and it's not true success.

Examine the extremes:

- Do what you love and no one pays you for it = Fun hobby at best
- Hate what you do and make a living (maybe even get wealthy) = Meaningless J-O-B and a numb soul

Be careful that the things you do support the end result you want…for yourself and your clients. Not every single task in your business will be a direct fit. Some paperwork has to be done, even if you hate it. But it's easier to swallow if you're doing what you want to do most of the time, and those other tasks support your doing it. In time, some of those less fun tasks can be outsourced to employees or contractors.

Pride and Narcissism

All this work to get inside your head and heart may feel a bit selfish at first. It can be, if you're building a business only to serve yourself.

However, if you are finding things that you enjoy that also serve others, it's not.

In order to give your best to others, you have to focus on yourself first. Then and only then can you identify what will bring out your best for others.

It's introspection, not narcissism.

Free to Give, Give to Sell

If you know what you want to get paid to do, you also know what you can give away for free. I don't care what your business is selling; there are always ancillary and tangential products or services that support your core product or service.

If you want to be a writer and sell books, perhaps you give away your speaking services (I know many authors who sell tons of books in the back of the room when they speak for free). But the opposite is also true...if you want to get paid to speak, you might want to give away your books.

And it isn't always as concrete as books and speeches. Shift the way you see your business: Are you selling the experience or the product? Are you changing people's lives, giving them pleasure, eliminating a problem, providing an essential service, or erasing an annoyance? Find the root of what you're doing for your customers.

No Jobs with Benefits

Chad Jeffers is a talented guitarist who has worked with such artists as Carrie Underwood, Keith Urban, and Kenny Loggins. In 2011, I met him at a party and he told us a story about pursuing your passion in work. He said that when he was growing up, his father told him that if he wanted to be a professional musician, he should never get a job with benefits.

His father had a decent job, and that sense of security kept him from giving 100% to his dream. Not every case is so drastic, but you can see the point.

What's holding you back from just going for it? Can you overcome that?

It may be hard, but if you want it badly enough I believe you can do it!

Play vs. Work

How do we differentiate between work and play? Can only play be fun and enjoyable? Does work have to be only about making money?

> A master in the art of living draws no sharp distinction between his work and his play, his labour and his leisure, his mind and his body, his education and his recreation. He hardly knows which is which. He simply pursues his vision of excellence through whatever he is doing and leaves others to determine whether he is working or playing. To himself he always seems to be doing both.
>
> – L. P. Jacks, *Education Through Recreation*

Most people need to conduct a deep evaluation of their view of work and play. Far too many see work as drudgery—a task required for sustaining life that has no life itself within. And yes, there are times in our lives where we may need to work simply for a paycheck. Just don't stay there forever!

While we're talking about it, let's look at getting paid. Is there anything wrong with enjoying something and getting paid well to do it? I don't think so. In fact, I believe if we build a plan, we actually can make more money doing something that we enjoy doing than doing something we hate to do.

It makes sense if only we would think about it. You've seen those people who hate their jobs. The scowl on their faces seeks only to bring your energy down to their level. They work at the end of long lines at the DMV or fast food restaurants. They are miserable and believe everyone else should be, too.

Smile at them and move on. You CAN find a way to make money and enjoy the work. You just have to work with that in mind.

Don't settle for work that isn't meaningful to you. I've worked for some miserable ogres in my time. They made me feel miserable. [Correction: I let them make me feel miserable. I stayed in those situations when I didn't have to. I put up with abuse that I didn't have to. I didn't cause it, but I allowed it to continue. Armed with that revelation, I know I won't allow it again.]

So can you play and get paid? Can you work and enjoy it?

Answer yes or put down this book until you believe it's possible…you won't get anything out of the rest of it if you can't wrap your mind around that one point.

Processes for Creating

Knowing that there exists a place (or places) where your desires intersect with where people are willing to pay you means you need to start building your roadmap.

Begin by documenting the things you enjoy doing. What would you be willing to do even if you weren't getting paid? Where do you lose track of time? What tasks or activities do you perform inherently well and enjoy?

Then examine where you do something of value and do it with excellence. What are people complimenting you on? Are people willing to pay you to do those things?

It may take some creativity. Some of those fun things are never going to result in a profit or at least not one you can live on. But that doesn't mean they aren't valuable inputs into the process.

Some things just aren't going to pan out as a job or a business.

Look for the intersections. Evaluate them. Which one looks the most promising? More importantly, which one makes you excited about the possibility? Explore them. Try them on for a test ride. Pick one and go for it!

Example Mission Statements

Below are a few example Mission Statements from my clients and students:

- Teach small to mid-sized businesses how to do marketing
- Create fun and artful international experiences that help people to move beyond cultural stereotypes and generic tourism and gain new perspectives on the world and humanity
- Aim to grow Christ's Kingdom through the fusion of ministry, mission and media
- Empowering and encouraging women to birth naturally
- Connect people to action sports year round, all day, every day
- I want to educate families about dog health and wellness through an active outdoor lifestyle

They vary in format, and many have additional context written into their SSP that is not included here. Use them to spark ideas for your own Mission Statement.

NOTE: *These are examples, not templates. Your Mission Statement may take any format you wish as long as it means something to you.*

SSP Instructions:
Mission Statement

The Mission Statement for your business taps into your passion and begins to define the dream. It should be succinct, clear, and unchanging. This is where you draw a line in the sand and give purpose to your business.

- **What does it exist for?** – Use your passion. Think about the reason you wanted to start the business when it was just an idea.

- **What will it always do, even if the products and services change over time?** – Think broader than the products and services you provide. Technology will change over time, and so will the needs and wants of your target market.

- **Start Writing** –Don't stare at a blank screen or sheet of paper too long. Start by writing down your thoughts, dreams, and desires for the business. Do mind-maps or other exercises to get going. Record yourself talking to a friend about it, and then take notes when you listen to it. Themes and keywords will start to appear.

- **Refine** – Once you get it down to a few words, review it frequently and refine it over time. Hopefully the concept will remain the same, but better words will punch it up.

SSP Step 2:
Mission Statement

What do YOU want to get PAID to do?

SSP Evaluation Questions:
Mission Statement

☐ **Does it feel good to you?**

This is a Mission Statement for you. It should excite you and get you going. But it should also feel good. When you read it or look at it, it should encapsulate all of the reasons you're doing this work. As Chuck Bowen always asks, "Will it cause you to leap out of bed every morning, eager to get working on your mission?" Share with your team, and if it's appropriate, with your customers.

☐ **Can you see multiple paths forward?**

At this point you don't need to decide the specifics of your business, such as what products and services you will offer (though you probably have some ideas already). The mission should be able to be fulfilled in multiple ways. Wear the mission for a bit and see what comes to mind.

☐ **Is there a market for it? Will people pay for it?**

Remember that we're talking about business, and business is about making money. Serve well and the money will come... if the market wants it and will pay for it.

☐ **Is it too specific?**

If it's all about a single product or service, it may be too specific. Look at the bigger industrial segment and then how your business is unique/remarkable in that segment.

Chapter 6:
Core Values

What does your business stand for?

People may survive for decades working in a job for which they have no passion. But few last very long if the job violates what they believe. It's even more pronounced if you own the business. If you don't believe in what you're doing, you're not going to be motivated to keep doing it with any level of excellence. It needs to stand for something—something you care about.

If you're going to fight for "truth, justice, and the American way," you'd better believe it and live it out. Anything less is untrue to your character and those you serve.

What Do You Care About?

As you look at the intersections of your desires and what is valuable to other people, you also need to look at the impact those activities can have on the world.

It could be that your idea has a direct impact that benefits a cause or belief you hold close to your heart. Maybe you start a charity that helps starving people or you build lightweight and affordable wheelchairs? Remember, it doesn't have to be non-profit to have an impact!

But maybe your idea doesn't have a direct impact. Sure, designing cool leather bags could result in people using them to carry medical supplies to people in need. But you didn't design them for that...you made them because they're cool. However, your heart and your passion are for kids in Africa. These bags make a lot of money. They attract a lot of attention. And so you funnel that money and that attention into the cause you care about.

That's a big part of the story of my friend Dave Munson and Saddleback Leather. Making the best leather products on the planet is enjoyable for him, but it isn't his mission in life. It simply funds his mission. Take note of that. His job (he owns the company) is making leather products. He enjoys it and going to work is not a burden. But he isn't so wrapped up in that "thing" that he ignores the greater call of his heart. They work together.

Changing the World

I have a strong personal need to have an impact on the world. I want to leave my mark, and I hope that mark is an improvement and not a stain or a scar.

In fact, this desire to have an impact is so great for me that I cannot imagine anyone not being attracted to it. But I understand that my impact will be manifested differently than yours. It's not about what we do to make an impact; it's that we make one.

Some will be visible. We will save lives or end wars or keep people from starving. Others will be more subtle or invisible to the world at large. We'll raise our kids to be strong and smart contributors to society.

I really do believe that everyone wants to change the world and make it better in some way. Go ahead and pursue that. Just remember that the impact we have isn't always evident. You may touch someone's life today, perhaps in an incidental or even accidental way. You may not know you did it. But it could set them on a course of change that radically alters their world and the world they interact with. Teachers and doctors and nurses and pastors do this all the time. The proof? Just ask them if they get letters thanking them from people they can't even remember.

Finding Bedrock

You want to build your business on a solid foundation. If it's unshakeable, it'll weather the inevitable storms that are coming (oh, yes…there will be storms!).

Establishing strong Core Values in the beginning allows you to more easily deal with adversity and opportunities. Core Values become a filter by which you can make decisions more easily. It becomes easier to say no to opportunities…or delay things that just aren't right for right now. And you can make wise decisions without difficulty, saying yes to the things that fit and no to things that don't.

Decisions from the Core

I have a friend who is an incredibly successful business owner. He has a massive audience and has helped many people. He was recently invited to participate in a traveling seminar series where he could share his message in packed auditoriums and sell a lot of books and products.

It was a very promising opportunity, and he met with the event organizers and attended one of their seminars. It didn't take him long to pass on the deal, and he had no regrets. Even though it likely would have led to hundreds of thousands of dollars in sales, he just didn't believe it was the right fit for his business.

From the outside, many people would think he was crazy. I even did for a moment! Most of us would jump in and not look back.

But he knew that if he did, he'd regret it later. Money wasn't going to be his primary motivator. He makes a lot, but it isn't an exclusive part of his Core Values.

In the end, this is how you keep your business true to the reasons that you start it in the first place. Nail it down now, making only minor adjustments as you grow and learn. This will allow your business to pursue the right opportunities with authenticity and integrity.

Core values are the banks that keep the river flowing.
– Jonathan Pool

Imagine you're just starting out, but have decided you want to cater to families with children. Then out of nowhere a big magazine wants to profile your product. The exposure will be huge! However, the magazine features scantily-clad women on its covers. Do you do the deal or not?

If you've firmly established your Core Values, you can pass on the deal without regret. It doesn't fit. You don't compromise your values and you continue to work on your business with integrity.

As you become more successful in your business, saying "no" will become harder. More opportunities will come around and temptations will surround you. You have to know what to walk away from, even if it's difficult.

Wrap your mind around this one: GE keeps its business units going only if they are #1 or #2 in a business category. If they can't be at the top of an industry segment, they sell it and leave it altogether. Can you define anything so absolutely that it drives your entire business?

Questions to Help Discover Your Core Values

Core Values express what you care about:
- What specific things in the Mission Statement do you want to make happen?
- Why do you want to be in business?
- What change(s) do you want to make happen?
- What product or service do you put out there to meet those ends?

But Core Values are more than just the product or service:
- What does your business value?
- What is it serving?

Core Values also help to define your target market. Focusing on serving a specific market vs. trying to sell to everyone will help you serve more people in more meaningful ways:
- Who do you want to serve?
- Why do you want to serve them?

Core Values define purpose. Business is about more than just making money. Make all you can, but use it according to your values. Be intentional about your use of money, because it will demonstrate what you truly value instead of what you say you value. Ask yourself:
- Where is that money going to?
- What will your business be known for? (It's bigger

than money.)
- How will you use your wealth?

Core Values can help define your business practices:
- Do you make it easy for customers?
- What do you promise them?
- What do you do if you fail to deliver... and does it reflect your defined values?
- Do you make and keep promises easily?
- How do you manage, lead and interact with your team?

Core Values can be whimsical! There is nothing wrong with adding fun as a value. Do things that keep you and your team excited about the work you do:
- Are there meaningless tasks that become more work than fun?
- How can you inject fun and enjoyment into the workplace?

Defining Your Core Values

Core Values create "no matter what" foundational statements. Everything that you do can be judged against these values. What you do must be in alignment with your Core Values...and while not all of the values apply in every situation, your efforts cannot be in conflict with them. Take your Core Values seriously, but don't be afraid to get creative.

Example Core Values

Below are a few example Core Values from my clients and students:

- Integrity is Essential: All dealings with clients and

prospects are conducted with the sincere intent of improving their situation without compromising my values.

- Profitability: I will provide products and services at a fair market value so that I can reasonably financially support my family and have margin for blessing others.
- Entertaining: People are receptive to new ideas when they are exposed to them in a fun and entertaining way. No boring lectures allowed.
- Be the foundation: My company exists like a coral reef, to be the foundation on which like-minded adults learn and communicate
- Flexibility: provide the guidance that my clients desire while being open to new needs and areas of opportunity (small businesses) that benefit from my message.
- I want my family and business to be surrounded by like minded people that will support one another and seek to change the current trend of depersonalized business.
- Fun: We are about having fun and providing fun experiences that stimulate the imagination and spark creativity.
- Quality: It is not enough to provide an experience. It must exhibit the utmost quality at every level of client interaction.
- Customer Service: We value every client and honor each as our guest. We handle every request, concern, and complaint promptly and with great respect.
- Honoring the God of the Bible: We enjoy the variety of people He has created and the cultures He has allowed them to develop, but worship only Him.

SSP Instructions:
Core Values

Define the Core Values of your business (the things you care about). These values will be specific extensions of the Mission Statement and define why you do it.

In the beginning it may be all about you. As you grow (if that's your desire), you may have other people working for your business. These are the values you want to instill in them, but also values you want to have defined so that when it comes time to look for employees, you already know what you want! It doesn't matter how talented someone is at a task...if they don't believe in your company in the right way, they aren't the right fit.

You may want to categorize the Core Values as Internal (what you value for yourself or within your business) or External (your values toward and on behalf of your customers).

These values will also allow you to explore the right opportunities to collaborate with other businesses and vendors. In order to stay true to your values, those you interact with will need to be in alignment with them as well.

SSP Step 3:
Core Values

What does my business stand for?

1	
2	
3	
4	
5	
6	
7	
8	
9	
10	

Download the SSP Template at ConquerYourKryptonite.com.

SSP Evaluation Questions:
Core Values

☐ **Do the documented Core Values represent who you are and what you want your business to be?**
Customers are savvy. They want a great deal, a lot of value, and an authentic experience. Be true to yourself and they will appreciate it.

☐ **Do they extend beyond your products and services?**
Core Values will be expressed through every interaction you have with your customers, and will also be reflected in how you spend and invest the money you earn.

☐ **Do they help to define your target market? Will they be attracted to your business if you follow them?**
Imagine the people you most want to serve. Ensure that your values honor them. They are people just like you!

☐ **Is your purpose expressed through these values?**
Your Core Values are an extension of your Mission Statement. They support the fulfillment of your mission.

☐ **Do your Core Values define how your business will operate and interact with customers?**
Stay true to your values in all aspects of your business.

☐ **Will they guide you through difficult decisions?**
Imagine a temptation or future struggle. Will the application of your values lead you to a positive final outcome?

Chapter 7:
Visioning

Dreaming Out 3-5 Years

It's time to dream big. This "little idea" you have may be huge! What would success look like if you could travel forward in time and observe yourself? Create the ultimate expression of your business over the next three to five years, keeping it realistic (but just barely).

X-Ray vision is cool, but it's better to peek into the future and find a way to make it happen. Fly in the direction you want to go.

Defining Realistic

I believe very strongly that your vision for the future has to be realistic. But that doesn't mean we build our vision according to all of the rules of our current reality!

I remember being in the first grade, amazed by and in awe of the third graders. They were big. They did big math. They had something I didn't have, and I didn't think I'd ever get it.

At that age, those third graders were about 20% older than I was. They had a two year head start, but that head start was huge!

However, I put in my time and two years later I was a third grader. I had achieved the pinnacle of success, right? Nope! There were sixth graders around now, and I wasn't as superior as I thought. The pattern continued year after year...there was always someone ahead of me, and I was always chasing them.

I don't chase them anymore. I chase myself instead!

I know that in the next two years I will be growing and learning. I'm feeding my mind and exercising my brain. I will be better *then* than I am *now*.

Therefore, the things I cannot do today are things I may be able to do tomorrow. And if that's the case, my possibilities are expanded. It's just a matter of how hard I'm willing to work.

So what is realistic? It's whatever you define as realistic. It's the cap on what you can accomplish. So be aggressive. Put it out there where it's kind of scary, like those third graders were in the eyes of a little first grader.

Warning: Don't let others define realistic for you. We never want to build it based on the reality someone else has created for you.

It's great to have the input and feedback of others we trust. Some will speak truth into our lives and we should listen to them. But some will steal your dreams if you let them. Don't let them.

More Than a Dream

A successful vision is more than a dream. Dreams are elusive and fuzzy.

Have you ever tried to tell someone about a dream you had the night before? What little you can remember is disconnected from reality and even other parts of the dream. It's disjointed and hard to convey the depth of the experience. Sometimes all that remains is a faint feeling with no understanding of why you feel that way.

But a vision...a vision is something that is tangible. You can describe it in exacting detail. And in doing so, you take one giant leap toward it.

> [I]f one advances confidently in the direction of his dreams, and endeavors to live the life which he has imagined, he will meet with a success unexpected in common hours.
> – Henry David Thoreau, *Walden*

Be Present in the Future

No matter the method used for creating the vision, it's always about being present in the future. We are imagining our lives in the future.

In the book *Build to Last*, authors Jim Collins and Jerry Porras coined the term "Big Hairy Audacious Goal" or BHAG. While intended for the strategic goal setting process, I believe it's a good fit for visioning as well. Put something out there that's impossible, then believe that maybe you can achieve it. More often than not, simply giving the impossible some attention makes it more possible. It may never happen, but you'll certainly learn from and be closer than if you didn't have a BHAG to begin with.

So let's pretend you've got a Delorean with a flux capacitor. Ramp it up to 88 miles per hour and travel to the future. Look around at everything you can see (but please don't interfere with the space-time continuum).

The idea is that you can begin to imagine the future you want, and in doing so, you can take steps to create that future. You can make it real. I'll show you how.

> It's kind of fun to do the impossible.
> – Walt Disney

Make Your Vision Tangible

Your vision deserves more than 11 words.

I have always struggled with the kind of vision statements that boil down the entirety of your dream into a few words. Not only does it make it difficult to differentiate from your Mission Statement, but it's totally dismissive of the process of crafting a vision. (If you must consolidate your vision into a few words, do it after this exercise.)

In February 2011, I found an article called *Creating a Company Vision* by Ari Weinzweig on the Inc. magazine website.[3] It radically changed my approach to visioning.

The author writes about his experience when creating a local farmers' market. His vision is three paragraphs and 380 words. It breaks all of the rules and I love it.

He literally frames his vision by describing the time of day, the state of the weather, the sights and sounds and smells and tastes as he walks through the market. It's worth reading, saving, printing, and hanging on the wall.

He invites anyone reading his vision to step into it and become fully immersed. This is more than a vision…it's future-casting. And three years later when he walked into the market for the first time, his experience matched his vision because his vision drove his actions.

---

[3] http://www.inc.com/magazine/20110201/creating-a-company-vision.html

I call it a Vision Narrative. Try your hand at this kind of vision. Make it big enough to be worth pursuing.

Write It Down

Write it down and stand in awe of the Vision Narrative. Once it's written down, you can make it happen. Likewise, if you can't write it down, there's no real chance you can do it. A written vision exists to encourage and inspire. It's also a reality check for the amount of work we have ahead of us.

A written vision is a tangible thing. It can be on paper, on a computer screen or in crayon. The key thing is that it becomes real to you. But there are other advantages.

When you write down your vision on paper it can be shared with someone else. Vague ideas about your vision will bounce around inside your head like a bullet. This is a dangerous place. The vision will never be born and the real world will never experience it.

First say to yourself what you would be; and then do what you have to do.
– Epictetus

Time to Go To Disney World

Your vision is about possibilities. It's taking your mind and your heart to Disney World.

This is the part where we have to resist the temptation to hold back. Go ahead and dream big! Ask a lot of "what ifs" that expand your dream (don't let them constrain it at all).

Tap into that eight-year-old that lives inside of your head and heart. Imagine what it would be like to walk into the Magic Kingdom for the first time. Feel that sense of excitement and write it down.

Vision Begets Action, Reality and Change

The next steps enter into action and reality…the how comes later, not when we build the foundation.

The vision needs to be attractive and challenging. It may be both a reality check and inspirational at the same time!

If it's not compelling, you'll be rethinking your business soon, or hesitating on everything. Passion will feed you and vision will direct you.

You need to be able to go forward with boldness and confidence. At the simplest level it's like pulling out of the driveway knowing where you're going to go out to dinner. It's easier if you have a destination in mind to begin with, but it's also easy to redirect if you have to. Going out without a plan is folly. You drive around in circles, going from hungry to starving until you give up and eat just about anything. This is not what you want for your business.

Casting a vision is a dynamic process. As you begin to document it, the vision may morph into something very different than what you thought at the beginning of the process.

This Planning Stuff Works!

One of the coolest things about the SSP is that I got out of the gray cloud that was surrounding and standing in front of me. Until I starting planning for my future, I could never see my future. It left me with fear, frustration, and an unclear vision. It was pretty scary and still can be, but once I got a plan the stresses became laughs. I believe life is easier to enjoy if you plan for it.

– Jonathan Tollefson, PARXbyJonT.com

Documenting Your Vision Narrative

There are actually three visions you need to craft.

- The first describes your vision for 3-5 years into the future. Don't be afraid to get wordy. I've had clients end up with a Vision Narrative that's two pages or longer. It belongs to you and it's for your use. Don't worry about condensing it to put on a plaque on the wall yet.

- The second vision describes where you are a year from now. Write it in the same tangible way you wrote the 3-5 year vision, but it can be condensed down to a few paragraphs.

- The third vision needs to focus on the next 90 days or so. Describe the things you've accomplished over the past three months, where you stand in moving toward your vision, and what your next steps are. A paragraph or two here will be fine. It doesn't need to be fancy.

Example Vision Narrative

Because the Vision Narrative is so intimate, I don't feel right sharing an example from my clients (several gave permission). Instead, I'll share a part of my personal Vision Narrative from when I first used this method several years ago:

> "It's December 31st, [3-5 years out from when I wrote it]. As my family prepares to celebrate the New Year, I'm reflecting on the past year and how far we've come. I'm finally living my dream of full-time self-employment. It wasn't easy, and it still isn't, but we've done it for a full year now and things are going well. My income is nearly what it was when I left my job, and the prospects for growing it in the next year are good.

Our home is a sanctuary. There is peace there. It is where we come together as a family and where I work.

My typical work days will start up again soon now that the holidays are winding down. When I'm in town, I'm able to wake up early and work before having breakfast with Heather and helping the kids get off to school. After a bit of exercise, I spend the mornings writing and developing products or speeches.

Some days I have lunch meetings, and afternoons are filled with client meetings and marketing for future engagements. I can generally shut everything down before dinner, then enjoy the evenings with Heather and the kids... just having family time.

On the days when I'm out of town, I focus on my clients. I enjoy the travel, but don't want to do it more than a few times each month and rarely for more than three or four days in a row. My trips are busy and intense—designed to minimize the work I have to do once I get home to my family.

I'm a professional author, speaker, trainer, coach and consultant. There is variety in my work, and I'm helping people follow their dreams and improve their businesses. There is a significance and impact in the work I do for others. They appreciate me and most of my business comes from their referrals.

I'm relaxed and content, but never lazy or complacent. I continually strive for that delicate balance.

My plans for the coming year are set. It's going to be an ambitious year. It's going to be a busy year. It's going to be a good year."

I haven't realized the entirety of this vision yet, but I'm closer than when I wrote it. Reading it still excites me, and I refine it at least annually to keep looking out 3-5 years so that I don't stop when I get there.

SSP Instructions:
Vision Narrative

A vision defines what's possible. It should be in line with your Mission Statement and will provide guidance for the actions you will need to take over the next 3-5 years. It will change over time (as your vision grows or is achieved), but should be firm enough that it doesn't change daily.

One way to start is to imagine walking through an ideal day 3-5 years in the future. Capture your environment and emotions:

- What do you do when you wake up?
- How do you interact with your family?
- What are your recent achievements?
- What tasks are you working on?
- What bigger dreams are you working on for the future?
- How do you wrap up your day?

In addition to documenting a long-term Vision Narrative of 3-5 years, craft a vision for about one year from now and a vision for where you want to be three months from today.

These shorter-term visions will begin to point out the work required to attain the long-term vision. Use these as your plan becomes more tangible in the coming steps of the process.

Your vision should be big enough to challenge you. Stand in awe of your vision, because once written, it's real and achievable.

SSP Step 4:
Vision Narrative

What do I want my business (and life) to become?

Long-Term (~3-5 years):

Mid-Term (~1 year):

Short-Term (~90 days):

Download the SSP Template at ConquerYourKryptonite.com.

SSP Evaluation Questions:
Vision Narrative

☐ **Does reading and sharing your Vision Narrative give you an emotional response?**

It should excite you, scare you, and put you to work! This is the written form of your dream. If it doesn't elicit some emotion, check your pulse and try again.

☐ **Is it tangible?**

Close your eyes and walk through your Vision Narrative. Use your senses to taste, touch, smell, see, and hear everything around you. It should offer a visceral experience.

☐ **Does it create a sense of awe or wonder?**

It should be big enough and attractive enough that it moves you into action. Your vision can't be small, easy, or boring.

☐ **Is it realistic?**

While it needs to create a sense of awe and perhaps even fear, it shouldn't be completely unrealistic. Slightly impossible is okay, but not absolutely impossible.

☐ **Do you believe in it?**

Many things are possible, but few are willing to do the work required to make them happen. If you have faith that there is a path forward that results in the realization of your vision, you can wake up each day and do the required work.

☐ **Did you capture three time phases?**

All three visions are important. The long-term vision makes the dream tangible. The mid-term and short-term visions break the dream into a believable, inspiring progression.

Chapter 8:
Business Objectives

Why does the business exist?
Outline the major initiatives for the business. Why does it exist? What is it meant to accomplish?

Success doesn't normally require saving the world. Know what you plan to accomplish with your superpowers.

What's Your Motivation?

If you've ever spent time with a four-year-old, you know that their favorite word is only three letters long: W-H-Y.

Four-year-olds are curious and have developed the capacity to explore not just the physical world but emotional and ethereal worlds as well. And when a four-year-old asks a question, every answer spawns another question. It takes time to peel back the layers and discover the root of their curiosity. It turns out those little versions of us have a layer of depth beyond their appearance.

As you explore starting a business, you had better spend a good bit of time exploring the root of your motivations. If you ignore this vital piece of your business' foundation, you'll find yourself out of balance very quickly.

Is it about making money? Sure, that's part of it and essential if you're going to build a sustainable business. But there has to be more or your business will be nothing more than a job.

Why do you want to start the business? What is the ultimate impact you want it to have? Why does it exist?

In other words, if you're going to spend 80-100 hours a week building and working in and on your business (it often takes that level of commitment in the beginning), what will make it worth it?

Play the game all four-year-olds play. Find someone to ask you why!

You need someone smart enough to help you peel back the layers of your motivation and get to the heart of why you'd want the headache and backache of running your own business. It won't be easy. But figuring this out at the beginning will help you decide if it will be worth it.

Measurements for Success

Once you have an idea of why your business exists (its ultimate purpose), you have to figure out how to measure your progress toward that goal.

Much like any other goal-setting exercise, you have to develop something that is specific and measurable. It should also be as objective as possible and may build in phases.

So you want to refresh the world? Figure out how many bottles of Coke that will take. Figure out how many you can do this year...and the year after...and the year after. Chart your progress and strive for that ultimate goal. It may be something that never can be fully attained...or can it?

This is your scorecard. This is what tells you if you're making progress or falling behind. This is what shows you when changes are needed or if you're doing the right things.

What to Measure?

Don't go overboard with data and metrics when you start developing the objectives. Have a sense of how they would be measured in simple ways. Some examples might include (with measurement comments in brackets):

- Become a recognized expert with a collection of raving fans, where half of new clients are based on referrals of prior clients within three years [track referrals over time]
- To build a sustainable and growing business that allows personal freedom and flexibility for me and my family [measure profit and growth, capture indicators of personal freedom (vacations, new family experiences, etc.)]
- To inspire and encourage those with untapped potential to see what they can accomplish and the responsibility they have to pursue their passions [track client success over time]
- To establish business relationships that are based on deep personal values that are more like family than corporate connections [measure client relationships that extend beyond business]

If you aren't measuring your progress, you'll eventually get far enough down your path that you lose sight of where you started, yet have no idea where you're going. That's when you lose.

Personal and Professional

When working with people, they almost always ask me if their plans—and specifically their Business Objectives—should be 100% business or if personal motivations should be included.

While there are times when you should focus more on true core Business Objectives, there really isn't a dividing line that makes sense when addressing your own business. You aren't an anonymous stockholder wanting to know projections for the next quarter. You're the quarterback driving the ball down the field. You're in it to win it!

So yes, include your personal motivations as much as your business motivations.

You want to be independent and build a business that supports you and your family without having to take a job or cut back expenses forever, right? Then that is a perfect business objective, and one almost all of my clients include in their plans. Gaining that independence allows them to engage fully in their business, which means they can engage fully in their passions. How can that not be good for a business that is properly aligned?

Time freedom also finds its way into most of my clients' plans. Who doesn't want to have more control over the course of their day? Sure, you may be working more in your business than you ever did in a job, but if you are able to choose your tasks and find enjoyment in them, it's worth it. You'll also be able to carve out time for non-business activities and family events that are important.

Label them as "personal" and "business" if you want to see the separation. It's not something I worry about because for me they are both important.

Core Values vs. Business Objectives?

Many of my clients initially struggle in determining the difference between Core Values and Business Objectives.

Try not to get too wrapped up in putting things into your plan in the "right" place on the template. Just like in the SWOT, it's more important that they are captured. No one is grading your SSP. Its value and effectiveness are scored by your success in executing the plan.

This may help frame the key differences:

- Core Values are statements of intention toward yourself, your customers and your team. They deal with how you treat and interact with people. They may also include aspects of faith and service.
- Business Objectives are more concrete and measurable. They outline your personal motivations for starting the business and the outcomes of the business. What kind of income needs to be generated? What kind of lifestyle needs to be created? How many products will you produce? How many customers do you want to reach?

What if it Didn't Exist?

Another good test for deciding your Business Objectives is to define what would not exist in the world if your business didn't exist.

If you're an inventor or product creator, that may have a huge impact if you're doing something that no one else can (or would) do in the way you'd do it.

For most of us, it's not that the world would miss out on our product or service. It's highly likely that someone else already has done it, is doing it or is getting ready to do it in one form or another. If Coke didn't exist, people would drink Pepsi or RC Cola. But it wouldn't be Coke, right?

This Planning Stuff Works!

The SSP helped me identify my "Why" as well as my "What." As much, or maybe more important than knowing what I was to do, was knowing why I was doing it—my motives and the outcome I was seeking.

The Mission Statement, Core Values, and Business Objective sections helped me to get clear and stay clear on my reasons for pursuing entrepreneurship. They were the fuel I needed to keep plugging away at my Action Steps when it seemed "nothing good was happening" or rather, just before the next good thing actually did happen.

– Melodie Kenniebrew, MochiInTheDesert.com

You are the secret ingredient to what you're working to do. It may not be that your product is any better or more special than any other on the market. It may be the way you serve or the impact you have on your customers. Zappos sells shoes online— the same shoes you can buy in most stores and even on other websites. What makes Zappos a powerhouse company is the way they treat their customers. They are a customer service business that happens to sell shoes.

The other factor to consider with this existence question is the hole in your heart. If you decided to give up on your idea at this instant, knowing that you'd never pursue it and never enjoy it and the world would never experience it, how would that make you feel? A nonchalant reaction here means you're not passionate about it. Though it may be worth pursuing, it's probably not the best fit for you. But if your heart breaks and you tear up a bit, know that you've found a personal connection with the idea. It's your baby and you have to carry it to term and raise it as your own flesh and blood. That's the kind of passion that will carry you through the 2 A.M. screaming fits and ER visits that are about to come.

Remember to ask yourself: What would not exist if you didn't go forward with your idea? What will exist if you do?

Example Business Objectives

Below are a few example Business Objectives from my clients and students:

- Be recognized as an expert authority on the National Level
- Be an invited speaker to relevant trade association meetings and conferences
- Generate a very comfortable living so that I can support our family and have margin to bless others radically
- Develop at least four streams of income including consultancy and workshop events some of which are passive streams of income
- Travel to other parts of the country and meet committed ethical business people
- Develop a personal network of like-minded entrepreneurs for support and growth
- Establish a firm web presence that encourages people to do something new that pushes them outside of their comfort zone and gives adventure to their lives
- Generate $50K in profits by 2019
- Connect women with professionals to help them with any needs they may have

- Be home with my children when they wake up, come home from school and be able to volunteer at their school for activities
- Travel every summer around the country leaving June 15 and returning July 30 – speaking engagements, visiting with family and friends!
- Become an online resource for business modeling in missions

SSP Instructions:
Business Objectives

List the specific things your business needs to accomplish. No more dreaming... these are future accomplishments!

Remember to document your motivations for starting your business (financial freedom, owning your time, brining a product/service into the world, etc.).

Capture both professional and personal objectives. They will support each other in most cases.

Be specific and outline the overarching goals for your business... even if it may take decades to realize some of them. Imagine the impact of your business on your life, as well as any impacts that may outlive you.

SSP Step 5:
Business Objectives

What is the purpose for my business? Why does it exist?

1	
2	
3	
4	
5	
6	
7	
8	
9	
10	

Download the SSP Template at ConquerYourKryptonite.com.

SSP Evaluation Questions:
Business Objectives

☐ **Do they connect with your motivations for the business?**
They should help to document the realization of your mission and vision. Once achieved, they point directly to why you started it in the first place.

☐ **Are they measurable?**
Some level of measurement will be needed in order to know if they are achieved.

☐ **Do they document the professional/business reasons you're starting the business?**
Capture the income and profit objectives, as well as things like the number of customers served.

☐ **Do they document the personal reasons you're starting the business?**
Capture desired changes in your life that the business can help to make happen. It could be related to family time, vacations, leaving a legacy, etc.

☐ **Have you captured the impact of your business?**
Remember to document why the business exists. Describe the change in the world (or a segment of the world) because you brought it to life.

☐ **Do they motivate you to get started?**
By now you should be excited to get to work. If these objectives are dull and flat, keep working on them.

Chapter 9:
Using the SWOT

Understanding your SWOT is a good first step... but it's time to take it to the next level. What specifically are you going to do to take advantage of Strengths and leverage Opportunities, or shore up Weaknesses and eliminate/neutralize Threats?

Superheroes develop Strengths, minimize Weaknesses, exploit Opportunities, and are always on the lookout for Threats. It's all just part of the job.

Let's Do Something With SWOT!

Remember the SWOT exercise from Chapter 4? Now that you've gained a greater perspective on what you're doing and where you're going by defining your Mission Statement, Core Values, Vision Narrative, and Business Objectives, you can start to apply the lessons from SWOT into your planning process. This is where we move from dreaming about your future to outlining specific actions to make it happen.

Begin by copying everything from your SWOT and pasting it into the SWOT analysis. I personally put each of my SWOT entries in italics, and then type up my analysis after the original text.

Each input on the SWOT should get a specific response. As you review each of your SWOT items, think about specific, intentional actions you can take. It's about being proactive and applying all of the observations you've made about yourself. You may discover new things to add to the list as you work through this exercise. Document them and respond as you complete this section of the SSP. The next few sections of this chapter will guide you through each quadrant of the SWOT.

Strengths: Use Your Unexercised Muscles

Everyone has Strengths. Unfortunately, we don't always do a good job of exercising and developing them into true talents. Even with a genetic predisposition to physical Strength, unexercised super muscles will not be as strong as exercised normal muscles. Put your Strengths to work and spend most of your time working out!

Think about each Strength and why it's a Strength. If it's listed because it's an area of excellence, write down how you can use that to your advantage. If it's listed because you have the talent but need to develop it, write down what you're going to do to turn it into a powerful force that you control as you go about your business.

Weaknesses: Don't Ignore Cracks in the Dam

Everyone also has Weaknesses and no matter what we do, we always will have Weaknesses. No one can be strong at everything.

If Weaknesses are ignored or unrecognized, they may be enough to cause us pain and failure. However, when we are proactive and build protections from our Weaknesses, we can prevent disaster.

Spend some time working on your Weaknesses and understanding how to keep them from harming your efforts. If you aren't good with numbers, you don't have to take accounting classes so you can manage your finances. Learn enough to get by and move on. Calculus is not required to balance a bank statement.

Some Weaknesses can be turned into Strengths, but that's rare so don't spend too much time here. Do enough to put it into quarantine and that's it. Having a basic level of competency in the essential areas is usually sufficient because you need to spend most of your time doing what you love to do and what you do well.

Invest most of your time maximizing your Strengths. You can outsource the rest. Hire a part-time bookkeeper to manage your finances if you hate doing it and/or stink at it. You'll spend a few dollars in the process, but save hours of frustration that you can use working in your Strengths instead—which is where your time earns the most money anyway.

Opportunities: Find Them and Use Them

If we look hard enough, there are more Opportunities than we can take advantage of at any given moment. Therefore we have to be intentional in pursuing only the best Opportunities.

Write them down. Evaluate them. Understand how to leverage them for your business. Just like a great idea, a great Opportunity will not manifest without action. Don't be passive. Seek out Opportunities and keep looking for them. New Opportunities tend to present themselves as we start making some progress. God blesses us when we start to move!

An Opportunity could be something you already have but are not using (a tool for making something, a friend with influential contacts, etc.). Or it could be the acknowledgement that such a tool or contact would be beneficial to your endeavor.

If you have it, how can you use it? If you don't have it, how can you get it? Your SWOT analysis is you telling yourself the actions that need to be taken to make and take advantage of an Opportunity.

Threats: Don't Be Blindsided

None of us can predict the future in a reliable and detailed manner. But we can be aware of the biggest Threats to our business. You've done the hard work of identifying the Threats against you already. Now put tools, processes and people in place to prevent those Threats from blindsiding you.

Not every bad thing can be prevented. But if you already know that something bad is possible, you can be prepared ahead of time and minimize its impact.

Potential negative impacts should be considered as you review your Threats. Something that would be absolutely devastating but is incredibly unlikely to occur probably shouldn't get as much attention as something that is highly likely but not full on Armageddon.

Perception and Reality

Building a SWOT on your own can be difficult. Your perceptions of yourself could be accurate, but will likely be biased (some of us in favor of ourselves, others overly critical). It's important to do two things to combat our own blind spots and biases.

First, share your SWOT and SWOT Analysis with friends, family, mentors and coaches. They can give you valuable feedback and correct any misperceptions. Their collective input is very valuable. If you rely on only one other person, you run the risk of their biases and misperceptions shaping you as much as your own do.

Secondly, continue to evaluate your SWOT as you work your plan. You are bound to have new discoveries and observations as you grow and learn new things about yourself. These new experiences will point out additional areas to change and grow.

SSP Instructions:
SWOT Analysis

Look back over your initial SWOT Analysis and develop specific actions to leverage your Strengths, mitigate/neutralize your Weaknesses, take advantage of your Opportunities, and eliminate your Threats.

Copy the contents of your SWOT and respond to each entry in detail.

Strengths need to be used or they offer no advantage. Put them into action. This is where you need to spend most of your effort.

Weaknesses can hurt you. Document ways to put them in a box or minimize their impact.

Opportunities need to be fed. Review each one and offer specific actions you can take to make the Opportunity a reality.

Threats will always exist and should not be ignored. Focus the bulk of your responses on those that offer the most immediate and severe impact. Often using your Strengths fully will minimize Threats.

SSP Step 6:
SWOT Analysis

	Strengths:
1	
2	
3	
4	
5	
6	
7	
8	
9	
10	

	Weaknesses:
1	
2	
3	
4	
5	
6	
7	
8	
9	
10	

	Opportunities:
1	
2	
3	
4	
5	
6	
7	
8	
9	
10	

	Threats:
1	
2	
3	
4	
5	
6	
7	
8	
9	
10	

Download the SSP Template at ConquerYourKryptonite.com.

SSP Evaluation Questions:
SWOT Analysis

☐ **Did you respond to each item from the first SWOT chart?**
Don't overlook anything that was already documented. Offer a proactive response to each entry. If it isn't worth a response, it isn't worth documenting in the first place.

☐ **Are your responses actionable?**
You must do more than hope or sit back and wait. Each entry should have at least one action you can take that will move your business forward.

☐ **Have you been honest with yourself?**
What you documented in your SWOT chart may look different at this stage in the planning process. Capture any changes or new entries and continue the process.

☐ **Are the responses realistic and meaningful?**
Don't document responses that you aren't willing to implement or are impossible to complete. If you write something down that you know is true, yet you are unwilling to do it, you have a bigger issue to deal with first.

☐ **Who is giving you feedback and advice?**
This is a very intimate, inside look at your business and your personality. It's easy to lose perspective in such an introspective process. Share it with other people that you trust in order to gain proper perspective.

Chapter 10:
Key Strategies

Must Do and Should Do Projects

Begin paring down all of the possibilities and look at what activities or projects will provide the greatest impact on your business in the near-term. What if you could work on only one thing... what would that one thing be? Get several of those "one things" and set them up as Must Do's... everything else falls to Should Do, only to be pulled in if other variables change or other projects are completed.

Save the kitten up a tree or stop an alien invasion? Picking your projects won't be so easy to rack and stack.

The To-Do Buffet... All You Can Eat with Wisdom

As a business owner, and especially during the planning and launching phases, you have a lot on your plate. It's almost as if you're standing in the middle of the world's largest buffet. Every food is gorgeous and delicious, and all of your favorites are there. There is so much to eat you don't know where to begin.

So you grab a plate and start piling it on. If you're really talented and don't mind your foods touching, you can stack that plate pretty high. Yet not everything you like or want fits on a single plate. You go back to your booth and chow down, already planning what to devour with your second plate.

The process continues until you are so stuffed you feel bad and question why you ate so much. It's a food hangover! You waddle to your car, promising never to return and to exercise in the morning, knowing that neither is likely to happen.

Running a business, much like the buffet example, is a never-ending collection of things to do instead of things to eat. Don't be Augustus Gloop (the very round German kid from the *Willy Wonka & the Chocolate Factory* movie).

I've had friends who had surgeries that restricted the capacity of their stomachs, either through banding or surgical removal of portions of the stomach. They are physically limited regarding how much they can eat. And when they go to a buffet, they use a smaller plate.

That's what we must do to gain control of the never-ending to-do's in our business. We have to have a smaller plate.

Understanding Projects

Entire books could be dedicated to defining what a project is and is not. Your experience with projects may be positive or negative, based on how you've seen the word used and/or abused through the years.

At the most basic level, a project is an effort undertaken for a specific purpose, with an intended outcome, and a clear beginning and ending.

A wedding is a project. The couple gets engaged and plans the details of the big day. The guests arrive, the happy couple says, "I do," and everyone heads to the reception before the newlyweds depart for their honeymoon.

Do you see the specific purpose, outcome, beginning and ending of a wedding?

It is much harder to define a marriage as a project. It has a purpose, but is there really a specific outcome? It has a beginning, and there eventually will be an ending—till death do us part—it isn't planned (though maybe there is a sad exception for pre-nuptials?).

For our purposes, a project is simply an effort that we must undertake for our business that is not as simple as a singular task but not so complicated that it never really ends.

Projects include things like creating a website, building a marketing plan or developing a new product. We may always be working in those areas, but by defining a specific version or release, we can impose an ending date and control our scope and efforts.

Understanding Priorities

We also must prioritize our projects. Just like the buffet example, there are simply too many things to do in the time we have available. If we try to do them all, we will end up accomplishing very little.

Some projects will be more important than others. So how do we decide which are the most important? While it can be difficult at times, it doesn't have to be.

The first thing you have to do is understand what projects are on your buffet. There will be a lot of them, so go ahead and write them down.

After you have them written down, look for themes. Use the themes to group together similar projects. Most people who are documenting projects actually start defining individual tasks. If one of your projects is to get a domain name, and another is to build your web pages, then you can legitimately combine those tasks into a project to create your website.

Top-Down or Bottom-Up Planning?

This chapter begins the process of defining Projects. The next chapters outline Goals and Tasks.

I tend to use a Top-Down approach, outlining my Projects first, and then the Goals for each project, followed by the Tasks required to meet each Goal. But you may think differently.

Many people are Bottom-Up thinkers. They outline all of their Tasks first, which point out the Projects and Goals required to meet their overall desires and objectives.

Both approaches work and can be used in the SSP planning process. Choose the method that seems most natural to you. But whichever method you use, try the opposite to evaluate what you've developed. It will help you find gaps in your plan that may not occur to you otherwise until well into the execution phase.

Once the projects are scrubbed and meet the criteria for a legitimate project (purpose, outcome, beginning and ending), begin putting them in order from most important to least important. Just pick two and rank them #1 and #2. Grab another and see if it's #1, #2, or #3. Keep going through all of the projects until none are left. There can be no ties.

What makes one project more important than another? The reasons may be objective and subjective. You can base it on getting quick results, higher profits, or just go with your gut. The important part is that some kind of rational ranking is established (it can always be changed later as events unfold).

Another thing to consider is precedence as you evaluate the projects. Some projects must be completed before others can begin, making a simple, low-profit project more important than a complicated, high-profit one. The preceding nature of the project gives it a greater importance. Don't put the cart before the horse!

Must Do vs. Should Do

With your ranked list of priorities in hand, now you can conduct an evaluation of your projects. Separate them into the projects you must do and should do.

The Must Do Projects are the things you need to be working on right now. They cannot be delayed. They will also tend to show quicker, fuller and more impactful results. These are the projects that have to be completed in order for other projects to be able to be started (precedence).

The Should Do Projects are everything else. They represent projects that are important, they just aren't as important right now. They may be more long-term, or require other projects to be completed before they can begin.

The time you have available to work on your business represents the size of the plate you are using when you go up to the buffet line. If you take on too much, you will accomplish less or feel overwhelmed in attempting to do it all.

The Must Do Projects represent your most favorite foods and cravings. You have a small plate, so you can't get everything, but these are the things you have to get while you can.

The Should Do Projects represent all of the other foods you enjoy on the buffet. You aren't ignoring them, though. You simply have to get through your first plate and see if there's any room left to go back for a bit more without overindulging.

Should Do Projects: The Holding Pen

The beauty of the Should Do Projects is that sometimes Must Do Projects finish ahead of schedule.

These Should Do Projects represent a grab bag of items you can incorporate into your schedule should time become available.

It also serves as an excellent holding pen for the ideas you get along the way. If a brilliant thought strikes your mind in the midst of your efforts, document it as a Should Do and keep working your Must Dos.

The new Should Do may be the top Must Do during the next planning cycle.

Project Duration

Some projects may take only a week to plan and execute. Others could take years. Some projects are driven by strict deadlines that define ending dates, while others will need to be given end dates.

At this part of the planning process, you only need to get a general sense of the duration of each project. Don't worry about conforming them to fit an artificial duration (90 days). The true duration of each project will come as we outline the tasks required to complete the projects.

SSP Instructions:
Key Strategies

This is the part of the planning process where you narrow your focus and begin to prioritize your efforts. There will be more things to do than are possible. Put your energy into the most important things and your business will have a fighting chance to survive and thrive.

Document your most important projects. Remember that a project has a specific purpose, an intended outcome and a defined timeline. Structure your projects accordingly.

Once documented, the projects must be prioritized from the most important to least important. This is a subjective process, but objective criteria may be used to help (impact, precedence with other projects, profit, timing, available resources, etc.).

Must Do Projects will get your immediate attention over the next 90 days, even if they may take longer to complete. These are the projects that typically have the biggest and most tangible Return on Investment (ROI)... which can be more than just money.

Should Do Projects are the holding pen for everything else you need to get done. Promote them as time or opportunities arise, but always act with intention. Some may never be realized, while others will be first in line for the next quarterly planning cycle.

SSP Step 7:
Key Strategies (Projects)

*What are the '10,000-ft-level' things I must do
to achieve my objectives?*

	Must Do Projects
1	
2	
3	
4	
5	
6	

	Should Do Projects
1	
2	
3	
4	
5	
6	
7	
8	
9	
10	
11	
12	

Download the SSP Template at ConquerYourKryptonite.com.

SSP Evaluation Questions:
Key Strategies

☐ **Does each Project have a purpose?**

> The purpose of the Project is bigger than the specific outcome of the Project. The purpose speaks to the impact the Project will have on your business, which goes beyond a product or service.

☐ **Does each Project have a specific outcome?**

> The Project must be realized. The specific outcome of the project must support its purpose. It may be a product or service, or it may prepare the way for products or services (infrastructure, elimination of roadblocks, etc.).

☐ **Does each Project have a beginning and ending?**

> Open-ended efforts are not projects. Dates frame your efforts and spark action.

☐ **Are your Must Do Projects the most important at this time?**

> Prioritizing your projects is a subjective process. Be intentional when ranking them and seek outside counsel from others who can challenge your assumptions and encourage your efforts.

☐ **Can your Should Do Projects wait?**

> Should Do Projects will not be worked on for at least three months. Can they wait that long? You can't do everything you want and need to do, and sometimes waiting on one project makes room for another to get completed.

Chapter 11:
Major Immediate Goals (90 Days)

Projects have specific outcomes and objectives. Some projects will fit within the 90-day planning cycle of the SSP, but many will not. Each Must Do Project should be segmented into specific goals for the next 90 days. If the project is completed in this time frame, that's great. But if it's a long-term project (more than 90 days), we need to set these goals in order to have meaningful and measurable progress as we move forward.

You can't fly faster than a speeding bullet...better have some milestones charted for the journey to see if you're on target.

Framing a Must Do Project into Goals

In Chapter 10 you learned how to outline your Must Do Projects. These projects require multiple actions to occur in order to bring them to reality.

Developing specific actions is defined in the next chapter. What needs to happen now is that specific Goals are defined that support the overall project and are limited to the next 90 days.

This is the Breakdown to Breakthrough aspect discussed in Chapter 3. The goals are simply the component parts of the overall project, for the next 90 days. **Goals are the glue connecting Projects and Tasks.**

Note that Goals should not exist independent of the Must Do Projects. If they do, perhaps you need a new Must Do Project or one of your Should Do Projects needs to be promoted to the Must Do list.

Anatomy of a Good Goal

Goals are going to break our projects into phases for the next 90 days. Perhaps the project can be completed in that time, but often projects will take more time. The Goals determine the effort to be expended only during this 90-day cycle.

If we look at a project to create and launch a website, then the Goal for the next 90 days may be to simply launch a static website for Phase 1, with a fully-dynamic web storefront in Phase 2 (Goals associated with Phase 2 may not need to be developed in detail, but it's good to have a sense of how they may drive Goals in the current cycle).

The timing of these efforts will be driven by the time you have available to work on it, the difficulty of the work, and/or the available budget.

There may be one or more Goals for each Must Do Project, just keep them at a very high level, describing the outcome, not the action to be undertaken. Within this context, I like to see the Goals as the "nouns" or tangible aspects of the project that will be accomplished in the next 90 days.

If the project won't take the full 90 days, then decide if it will be accomplished at the beginning of the phase or the end. If other projects in the 90-day cycle are dependent on it, then it may need to come early. If it's a lower-priority Must Do Project, then pushing it back may allow you to focus on the other higher-priority Must Do's first.

The next chapter will describe how to create very specific tasks and deadlines for each Goal, which will build out the timeline for your efforts.

Theory of Triple Constraints

All projects have three major components:
1) Schedule (how long will it take?)
2) Cost (how much will it cost?)
3) Scope (what will the outcome be?)

When the project plan is first drafted, all three are in balance and limited based on the assumptions built into the plan. (Generally only two of the three are set where desired… the third is accepted based on the other two.)

Once work begins on the project, things change. An adjustment to one of the three components forces a change in the others.

For example, if the project is behind schedule, it can be corrected by increasing the cost and/or reducing the requirements to be accomplished (scope).

My personal observation is that when a project nears completion, it's harder to adjust the components. At that point, it's no longer a choice between which of the three will be changed. It's now which one (if any) can remain unchanged. This is normally very painful for the project manager and key stakeholders.

The point? These three components are connected... and things will change so be ready to accept that fact as you execute your projects.

The Boundaries Narrow

As you define the time it will take to complete each Project and Goal, you'll quickly be able to see the amount of time it takes to complete everything on your plate. Time is limited and you may need to make hard choices once you begin to work your plan.

That's okay! Just keep focused on making forward progress with the most important priorities. Most first time planners are too aggressive and bite off more than they can chew. As long as you are farther along than when you started, the process has been successful.

As you continue to work through this planning process, one 90-day cycle at a time, you will understand how you work and how much you can or cannot accomplish in that amount of time.

SSP Instructions:
Major Immediate Goals

Copy each of your Must Do Projects into the template and document the Major Immediate Goals for each one.

Immediate is the key word. Planning too far out can be paralyzing. Instead, focus on the next 90 days and define the specific things you need to achieve to move your business forward.

Some of the Projects will be completed within the 90 days, while others will take longer. Document only the Goals that can be completed within 90 days.

Create a sense of urgency and build some momentum! Be aggressive, but realistic in terms of your resources (time, money, etc.).

Your Goals should be specific and measurable. Write them in terms of the accomplishment to be achieved, not the action of doing them (noun-based instead of verb-based).

Each Project will need at least one Goal, and most will require several to be accomplished.

SSP Step 8:
Major Immediate Goals

Project 1	
Goal A	
Goal B	
Goal C	
Project 2	
Goal A	
Goal B	
Goal C	
Project 3	
Goal A	
Goal B	
Goal C	
Project 4	
Goal A	
Goal B	
Goal C	
Project 5	
Goal A	
Goal B	
Goal C	
Project 6	
Goal A	
Goal B	
Goal C	

Download the SSP Template at ConquerYourKryptonite.com.

SSP Evaluation Questions:
Major Immediate Goals

☐ **Can the Goal be accomplished within the next 90 days?**
Remember that the Project may take longer, but the Goals are framing the work within your 90-day cycle. It's okay to be aggressive and ambitious, just keep the effort within the cycle.

☐ **Will it be easy to know if the Goal is completed?**
Vague Goals do not move us to action and completion. They are dreams without a plan. It's time to get specific if you're going to have accomplishments at the end of 90 days.

☐ **Is it more of a Task or a Goal?**
Goals are an expression of the future achievement. Keep them noun-based. Verbs are action words that will be used in documenting your Tasks.

☐ **Does it advance the purpose of the Project and help move it to completion?**
Goals are children of the Project. They must reflect the purpose of the Project and support its completion.

☐ **Does every project have at least one Goal?**
A Project without a Goal lacks purpose and a specific outcome. The Project may not be a Project, but an expression of desire or need. Rework the Project and the Goals will become clear... and the desire or need can then be met.

Chapter 12:
Action Steps

Based on the outlined Goals, it's time to create a breakdown of tasks that drive them to completion. For each Goal, document a series of Action Steps to include due dates, resources and assignments... then make them happen. This is where the work gets done!

Action heroes take action. This is where all of their training and preparation get put to good use. It's time to get going, one step at a time.

One Bite at a Time

Verbs are action words and that's what we want to create as we plan our Action Steps. Look at each Must Do Project and its Goals, and then simply outline all of the actions it will take to complete them.

What we are building here is a very clear hierarchy or work breakdown structure (WBS). At the top is the Must Do Projects, followed by Goals and then Action Steps. It looks like this:

Must Do Project
- Goal 1
    o Action Step 1
    o Action Step 2
    o Action Step 3
- Goal 2
    o Action Step 1
    o Action Step 2
    o Action Step 3
- Goal 3
    o Action Step 1
    o Action Step 2

These Action Steps need to be bite-sized efforts. Most will require a very finite amount of time and work. If you need to purchase a URL for your website goal, then that's all you have to do. "Purchase URL" is your task. That task could be broken into or include other tasks like researching domain providers, analyzing pros/cons, and making a selection before making the purchase. You could go wild and document it down to each click it takes to make the purchase, but taking this simple plan down to that level will steal your progress.

The level of detail needed in the plan will vary by the type of task and the type of planner. Do the minimum needed to get the job done and remember that getting the job done is the most important thing. We need to get to action, and not plan ad nauseum.

But What If Action Steps are Easier To Document?

Many people find it easier to document their detailed Action Steps before outlining their Must Do Projects and Goals.

There is nothing wrong with this approach! Just don't ignore the importance of having defined Projects and Goals.

Do what works for you. However, make sure that you're getting positive and improving results, and that you are willing to experiment occasionally to see if there are better ways of getting things done.

To help ensure I haven't missed anything, I'll look at the final plan from both perspectives. I almost always make adjustments when I do this.

Understanding Sequencing

Just like there was a certain order to the Must Do Projects, there will be an order to the Action Steps. If you were baking a cake, you wouldn't turn on the oven before buying the cake mix.

Document all of the Action Steps and then simply look for a logical order to get them completed. Unless you are developing a very complicated project like in construction or manufacturing, you shouldn't need to document all of the items' predecessors and successors. Keep it simple.

Initially all you need to do is document the sequence of the Action Steps. Timing and resources can be developed after the basic structure is completed.

Setting Due Dates

Due dates are significant features of a good Goal and the principle remains when it comes to your Action Steps. We're at the end of the planning process, and we can have everything else nailed down. We can know every little task that has to be completed. But if we don't DO the work, it won't matter. Setting deadlines injects action into the process.

Every Action Step must have a due date. It's the only way to know when they should be accomplished.

Most Action Steps also need a start date (depending on how detailed your plan is going to be). With a start date and end date, you know the duration of the task. It may only require one hour per day, but could take five days to complete. Knowing the full duration and the time allotted to each Action Step gives you a better picture of your plan's workload requirements. Whether your plan is realistic or not begins to shine through once these details are in place.

I like having start dates because they allow me to see which Action Steps are active for each week. And because some Action Steps could take multiple weeks, focusing only on the end date could lead to ignoring them until the final week. That's just institutionalized procrastination on a massive scale!

Advanced Technique: Critical Path

What if you have a very complicated set of Action Steps to be sequenced? It may be time to formally link the Action Steps to one another and uncover the critical path.

The critical path is a basic project management technique to discover the fastest possible path from beginning to end. With start dates and end dates for all Action Steps, and Action Step dependencies documented, the project plan will show the sequence of Action Steps with no slack (tasks with no room for delays). Resource availability can also factor into the calculation of the critical path.

Knowing the Action Steps that have slack helps you move things around, forward or backward, in order to manage your workload and the resources at your disposal. It's also important to have documented slack when project efforts start to fall behind schedule. That slack can sometimes be used to catch up by shifting priorities and resources, though normally a slip in critical path tasks mean a slip in the project (and your project sponsors and stakeholders will want to know exactly how big the delay is going to be).

Why do I not include it in the SSP? Because it isn't simple and it isn't needed as much for the individual nature of the SSP. Just put your Action Steps in the order they need to be accomplished and enough of the dependency will shine through.

Managing Resources (People and Things)

For many people reading this book, every Action Step outlined in the plan will be assigned to one person: YOU!

But that isn't always the case. You may have employees who can work specific items. You may hire a coach or a contractor (web designer, accountant, etc.) to work through the Action Steps.

Regardless of who is assigned to work an Action Step, it is important that an assignment is made for every single Action Step. If no one is assigned, then no one has ownership and no one will end up doing it.

Additionally, you may require certain tools or equipment to complete a task. Documenting these items as a part of the Action Step will help ensure that you don't forget about them when you set out to work on the task.

Concrete Assignments

If you do have more than one person working from your plan,

make sure that everyone understands exactly what is expected of them. This is needed so that Action Steps are completed efficiently and effectively, with as little confusion as possible. The plan itself —when it's simple enough for all team members to understand— becomes a great communication tool.

Most Action Steps should be broken down into components by individual so that there are no misunderstandings about who does what. The larger your team, the more important this is.

Clarity, clarity, clarity! As the business owner and planner, you assume the role of project manager. Act like it! Manage the project actively and intentionally.

> If you have built castles in the air, your work need not be lost; that is where they should be. Now put the foundations under them.
> – Henry David Thoreau, *Walden*

Level of Detail for the Planning Cycle

How much detail is required when building out the Action Steps?

Personality and patience will play a large role. I would recommend that high-level Action Steps be documented for the entire 90 days. Detailed Action Steps should be planned for the next 30 days, so that a week-to-week plan can be developed, at a minimum. A daily plan can exist and will work for some, but for most weekly will be fine.

The trick here is that a lot of work and effort is put into making this plan. Don't waste that effort! Review your weekly plan often, daily if possible, so nothing is ever missed. Know the actions you have on tap for the week and what work you can give to them each day. Do the work and you'll see the results week after week after week.

SSP Instructions:
Action Steps

Copy each of your Must Do Projects and Major Immediate Goals into the template, and then define the actions needed to accomplish each Goal.

Every Goal will have at least one Action Step (likely more). Set start and end dates, assign resources, and get to work!

When you first start this process, it's hard to know how long things will take and how much effort is involved. It's a BIG guess, but you will learn and make adjustments along the way.

Consider this advice from one of my students, Victoria Jones of OutstandingLandings.com, as she finished her first SSP cycle:

1. **Factor in extra time for action steps requiring work with other people.**
   Their schedule is not necessarily the same as yours.
2. **Factor in extra time for learning curves.**
   They may be much steeper than anticipated. (I really underestimated the learning curve for setting up a website!)
3. **Factor in extra time for life.**
   Stuff happens!

SSP Step 9:
Action Steps (Tasks)

Project 1*				
Goal A				
	Action Steps/Tasks	Name/Resource	Start	Finish
1				
2				
3				
4				
5				
Goal B				
1				
2				
3				
4				
5				
Goal C				
1				
2				
3				
4				
5				

*repeat for each project

Download the SSP Template at ConquerYourKryptonite.com.

SSP Evaluation Questions:
Action Steps

☐ **Is each Action Step actionable?**

Action Steps should usually begin with a verb. This will make it action-oriented before you even begin.

☐ **Are start and end dates listed?**

Dates will help define your schedule of activities for the next 90 days. Some may last a day or less, while others may take weeks to complete. Knowing which tasks are on your plate each week ensures you know how to use your time.

☐ **Are resources assigned?**

Writing your name down on solely-owned Action Steps emphasizes personal responsibility. If an Action Step involves other people, put their name(s) down so that you know to engage them to get it done. It's your business, so it's your responsibility.

☐ **Review your plan. Is it impossible?**

It's easy to bite off more than you can chew. Now that it's written down, it may be overwhelming. But is it impossible? It needs to challenge and push you. But if you're already set up for failure, reevaluate your Projects, Goals and Action Steps to make it more realistic.

☐ **Is your plan flexible?**

This is your plan for the next 90 days. It will change as you begin to execute. Be okay with that and keep moving forward.

PART THREE

EXECUTING THE PLAN

Your plan is pointless if you don't put it into motion. It's time to go!

Part Three outlines some of the tools, techniques, and lessons I've learned through my work as a project manager, business consultant, and coach.

Some of the concepts may inspire changes or additions to your plan. Be flexible enough in your planning to not only look for those changes, but welcome them. It will improve your plan and its chances for success.

Chapter 13:
Plan-Do-Review-Adjust

No plan survives contact with the enemy. No matter how good the plan, it is bound to be derailed by poor assumptions, bad estimation, unforeseen Threats or even unexpected Opportunities. Once the Plan is being put into action (Do), take time to Review it, evaluating what is working and what is not. Don't be too quick to change everything, but once a trend is identified counter it or take advantage of it (Adjust). Rinse and repeat as you continue to plan and execute over and over again.

Kryptonite comes back in surprising ways. No plan can eradicate it completely. Some plans go wrong and even grow Kryptonite. Deal with it wisely.

Contact with the Enemy

With a completed plan in hand, you sit down to execute the first task on the first day and find...resistance! For some reason, things don't go as planned. Some tasks take longer, or cost more money or simply don't work. Is it time to scrap your plan and start over? Probably not.

The reality of planning is that most plans don't survive contact with the enemy. The enemy in this case is simply the fact that you can't know everything so completely or precisely as to have a perfect implementation. In other words, the enemy is real life.

But real life doesn't mean we shouldn't plan. In fact, it means that it's more important than ever that we have a plan. There are distractions and obstacles everywhere. If you go through life without any plan at all, you'll probably end up accomplishing only accidental things. **I want more than just accidental success.**

By following a simple process as you build and work on your plans, you can see how to give time to an effort in the face of resistance, as well as when it's time to make massive changes to your approach.

Without a plan, most people simply Do and Adjust. They do something and constantly change it (or quit it for something else). This two-step process is better than not doing anything at all, but it results in a lot of random activities and limited results. It's easy to make knee-jerk reactions with a process like this, because as soon as something isn't working or isn't comfortable, it's easy to go in a whole new direction.

We've already addressed the need to add a Plan to the cycle. Planning is the first step and creates the foundation from which we will execute. But planning, doing, and adjusting misses a critical component...learning from our results. Therefore, we have to add a Review to the process. We need to evaluate our results and re-evaluate our plans. What works and why? What doesn't work and why not? Has our vision shifted and are our actions still in line with the Vision Narrative? Has the market shifted, and do we need to shift with it?

This Plan-Do-Review-Adjust cycle[4] is a critical method that, when applied intentionally, will keep us on track and up to speed.

Making Things Happen

The first two sections of this book address why we need to plan and how to build a plan. Now is the time when we talk about putting things into action. We need to move into a new phase in our process—the phase of doing!

If you've planned properly, you have created a collection of Projects, Goals, and Action Steps that align with your Mission Statement (purpose), Vision Narrative (dream) and Strengths (talents). It should account for the time you have available over the next three months and can be broken down into weekly tasks.

This is where the entire process becomes really simple. Go do those tasks. That's all. Just work the tasks for this week that you said you were going to do. Those tasks should support the accomplishment of everything you wanted to do. Progress may be slow, but if you do them you should be advancing in the direction you want to move.

As you head toward your goals, be prepared to make some slight adjustments to your course. You don't change your decision to go — you do change your direction to get there.

– Zig Ziglar, *See You at the Top*

---

[4] The Plan-Do-Review-Adjust cycle is my take on the Plan-Do-Check-Act (PDCA) process developed in large part by Dr. W. Edwards Deming. To learn more, visit http://en.wikipedia.org/wiki/PDCA.

The Resistance[5] will be there, too. It will make some things harder than they should be. Just press forward and do all that you can. Remember your Vision Narrative; review it often as a reminder of why you're working so hard. Press through and continue to work your plan as closely as possible. Minor changes may be needed, but don't give up on a task or effort too quickly. Some simply need time to start getting results.

> A good plan, violently executed now, is better than a perfect plan next week.
> – George S. Patton

Patient Review

Toward the end of your three months of execution, it's time to start building the plan for the next three months. You've learned a lot about what works and what doesn't. Some things probably changed along the way, but now is the time to make big changes.

Think about what worked well and how you can do more of those things. Why did a task go well? Was it because of your talents or Strengths? Was the timing perfect? Did it get results that exceeded your expectations?

Think about what didn't go well and how you can do those better or perhaps not at all. What tasks can be eliminated? If it's a waste of time, don't do it. What else can you do instead that will get the results you want or need? Understand why a task was not productive. Once you do, you know what needs to be changed in order to give it a chance for success.

---

[5] If you haven't read *The War of Art* by Steven Pressfield...go get a copy and read it as soon as possible.

Appropriate and Timely Adjustments

There is no clear-cut rule to say when an adjustment needs to be made. You will have to evaluate, based on your prior experience and expectation of future performance, which tasks need to stay the same, which need to be changed, and which need to be eliminated.

While we have a three-month, intense planning cycle built into our plan, the plan itself stretches beyond a mere 90 days. It is an attempt to focus our long-term efforts into a shorter time period so that we can make small steps in the right direction.

When planning the next 90-day cycle, review all of the Action Steps (completed or not). Learn something from each one. For those that were completed successfully, what could have been done differently to make it better? Apply those lessons as you plan again.

If an Action Step failed, it's important to understand why. Perhaps the method used was the wrong one. Or perhaps it's just not possible. But don't give up on it until you evaluate it and find some new understanding. That understanding will allow you to change your approach and meet the overall objective in a different way.

There is no substitute for persistence....
Failure cannot cope with persistence.
– Napoleon Hill, *Think and Grow Rich*

For Action Steps that remain incomplete, evaluate why they were started and not finished. Was significant progress made even if they weren't fully accomplished? Did outside forces influence them, causing overruns of time or budget? Did other Action Steps take priority over them, or did you not give them the priority they needed and deserved?

With some basic evaluation of the activities from your prior planning cycle, you'll have significant inputs for the next one. Every incomplete, abandoned and failed task should be considered for the next planning cycle...some will make the cut and others will get cut.

Rinse and Repeat

The Plan-Do-Review-Adjust cycle is never-ending. You will always need to build your plan, work your plan, assess your results, and make changes. The process is perfectly designed to fit into a three-month cycle, which gives you enough time to work on a concrete set of tasks while giving them enough time to see if they produce the desired results.

Adjustments should be made between cycles, and there are four cycles per year. At the end of each year, do a deeper review and make more significant adjustments. After multiple cycles, you'll have a pretty good sense of what needs to change and how to change it.

Chapter 14:
One Thing at a Time

The evil of multitasking pervades our society. The seeming ability to juggle disparate priorities with ease is applauded wherever we go. But the stunning truth is that people cannot truly concentrate on more than one thing at a time. The more balls you are juggling, the harder you have to work to juggle any of them well. Go deep with one thing before moving to the next.

Real life superheroes have mastered the powers of concentration and focus. But lasers still don't come out of their eyes.

Multitasking is a Myth

If only you could watch yourself trying to multitask! Reviewing the tapes, you'd see (even without slow motion) the foibles of trying to do more than one thing at a time.

As I was writing this section of the book, I tried to open a bottle of water and take a drink while clicking a pop-up on my computer. As the pop-up loaded, I was twisting the cap. I lifted the drink to my lips with my right hand while starting to move my mouse with my left (I'm right handed).

In this awkward attempt to do two things at once, I realized that I actually was doing only one at a time. The drink paused at my mouth when my focus moved to clicking the mouse. Once I clicked, my focus returned to the drink and my thirst was quenched.

I got lucky and didn't spill it all over my shirt! Had that happened, I have a friend who would have called it multi-failing (while laughing at me)!

It would have been far more efficient to finish taking my drink before closing the pop-up. But even with this knowledge, I still fall into the multitasking trap. It takes intentional effort to focus on just one thing at a time.

Power in Concentration

People can walk and chew gum at the same time. But those are low-level tasks (they don't require a lot of brain function). I'm talking about the tasks that mandate focus and concentration; things you can't do while on autopilot.

Habit and experience can make a complicated task easier, allowing the appearance of multitasking. However, any task worth doing is worth doing right, and doing it right means applying the right amount of effort with focus and concentration.

Let's be intentional in our efforts that matter. No more autopilot. It's time to take control of our actions and give them the focus they deserve.

100% Concentration

It's not hard to do two things at once. I'm a big believer in letting my laundry run while I do dishes. But it would be a disaster to actively do my laundry and dishes at the same time.

So line up your Action Steps and see what you can have going on simultaneously. Just understand that you can give your attention to only one thing at a time.

Think I'm wrong? Try concentrating on a movie or sporting event you care about while your spouse or kids are asking you questions!

Light Bulb or Laser?

Think a moment about light bulbs. By sending light out in all directions, they brighten an entire room. They also generate heat, but an ordinary light bulb doesn't generate enough to make you sweat or keep you from entering a room. They are pleasant and helpful.

Contrast that with a laser. A laser is made up of light, and at the most basic level, it's the same light that brightens a room. The difference is that a laser's light has been harnessed. It's been focused. It moves in a singular direction. And that same light that brightens a room, if concentrated enough, can cut through steel.

The difference between a laser and a light bulb can serve as an analogy for our focus when working on tasks. Analyze the tasks you have to do and decide if your effort (concentration) requires a light bulb or a laser.

For routine tasks like vacuuming or doing dishes, a light bulb is probably sufficient. You can listen to music or talk to someone while you're doing the job. It could be called multitasking; your efforts are divided between background functions and a primary activity (just like the light bulb's light is diffused).

But what if you're sucking dirt out of the carpet and see your wedding ring in the path of the vacuum? I doubt you hear the music playing even though it hasn't stopped. Your attention is focused like a laser as you divert the vacuum or turn it off to save the ring.

That's the power of a laser-like focus. In an instant, you harness all the powers of your concentration in order to accomplish a single mission. Specific tasks require a level of focus that multitasking just cannot compete with.

There's another aspect of lasers and light bulbs that applies when thinking of our tasks. Lasers require a lot of energy. They generate a lot of heat and the more intense the laser, the more it can do (or the less it needs to be used).

Harnessing all of the powers of your concentration is hard. It can be exhausting. You cannot operate in hyper-focus mode every minute of every day. The calmer and quieter "light bulb" routine activities are times to recharge, yet meaningful progress is still being made.

Set aside a specific time to work on important activities with a focused effort toward a specific result. Need to write a chapter of your book or develop a presentation? Shut out everything else and focus! If this is especially hard, start with just five minutes of singular focus. Just like muscular strength, concentration must be exercised and can be grown.

Dealing with Distractions

Our modern world is full of distractions. But even a farmer 200 or 2,000 years ago had distractions to keep him from his work. How can we keep and maintain our focus in the face of these distractions?

The most important step is to recognize what our greatest distractions are. Is your greatest distraction other people? Perhaps you need to be alone more. Is it the internet (Facebook, Twitter, email, etc.)? Shut it off for a while.

Once you understand what is stealing your time and attention, you can change your behavior to get better results.

Tracking Your Time

One technique that will help you understand how you work is to complete a time budget. Dan Miller introduced me to this technique. All you do is create a grid that breaks your day into 10-15 minute sections. For a period of time, at least a week or two of typical work, document everything that you worked on for each of those segments into specific categories based on the type of work or distractions you have. Spend an hour writing a proposal? Put it down. Waste an hour browsing YouTube videos? Put it down.

At the end of the period, you'll have a pretty decent idea of where your time is going. You will be amazed that some tasks take up so much time yet yield tiny results. You can then use this data to be more intentional. Put limits on the time you'll spend on unproductive tasks. Put specific time into your schedule for the most important tasks.

Dan uses this technique every year to evaluate himself and ensure his activity is aligned with his intentions. Brilliant! Learn more from Dan at 48Days.com.

> Often success in goals comes not by adding more to our busy lives, but by deciding what we're going to stop doing.
> – Dan Miller, *Wisdom Meets Passion*

The Pomodoro Technique

Another powerful method to focus your time and attention is called The Pomodoro Technique. It basically involves using a timer to set aside 25 minutes for intense activity on your most important tasks. After the time is up, take a five-minute break before starting another 25-minute surge of focused activity. After four 25-minute sessions, you take a longer 15-20 minute break before starting again. You can learn more about it online at PomodoroTechnique.com.

Lead Your Life from Quiet

My friend and coach Kent Julian has a wonderful approach to keeping his tasks aligned with his intentions.

Each morning he wakes up and begins the day with what he calls the 6 B's: Body and Brew (exercise and coffee), Bible and Prayer (study and prayer), Blessings Journal (five minutes of documenting something he's thankful for), Books (learning), Big Picture Thinking and Planning (reviewing plans and building for the future), and Block Out the Day (an intentional approach to the day ahead). For full details visit LiveItForward.com/6-bs-lead-your-life-from-quiet/.

Kent focuses his efforts on the 20% of tasks that get 80% of his results, with a daily focus on the 1% that is most important. You can learn more about Kent and his methods at KentJulian.com or LiveItForward.com.

Experiment!

No method will work for everyone. Whatever the technique you use to gain some focus from distractions, just make sure it works for you.

Chapter 15:
Prioritization and Daily Action

Being overwhelmed is normal if you want to accomplish anything large and worthwhile. Even with a good plan, the temptation to multitask and bounce from one thing to the next to the next to the next is ever-present. You are your own SOS if you have Shiny Object Syndrome, bouncing from one random task to the next. Instead, begin each day and week and month outlining the three to five things you are going to do (or not do). Evaluate yourself at the end of the day and see what you've been able to accomplish.

Superman has a purpose and he lives it out daily—even when he's Clark Kent. After all, there are deadlines to meet at the *Daily Planet.*

Being Overwhelmed

The last chapter dealt a lot with multitasking and being distracted. If you don't find some focus and attention, you'll move quickly into the next area of un-productivity: being overwhelmed.

It's easy for it to happen. You bite off more than you can chew, either in your plan or with family or other commitments. There are only 24 hours in a day, and some of them have to be used for sleep and relationships.

You Can't Work All of the Time!

I know that's really obvious and I almost deleted it, but it needs to be said. I'll say it again:

You can't work all of the time!

Some people just need to see the words in print. If that's you, I suggest you put it in your own handwriting and post it where you'll see if often (monitor, bathroom mirror, refrigerator door, etc.).

The truth is that I'd rather you be a little overwhelmed than a little underwhelmed. Having a bit too much to do can spur you to action and spawn creativity. But be careful. You can't operate in the red-zone constantly. You will end up exhausted and frequently crashing until you recover enough to reenter the field of battle. If that happens, you aren't being efficient or effective…you're merely surviving.

So use a little bit of overwhelm to help push, but don't stay there too long.

Picking the Daily Poison

With each day limited by time and our energy level, how do we know what the most important thing to do is?

This isn't scientific, but it's often the thing you least want to do. Get those tasks out of the way as early and as quickly as possible. If you do the easy or fun things first, the looming nasty one will rob you of the enjoyment of the others. Take on the challenge, defeat it and move forward. The rest of the day will seem easier.

> [Y]ou have to decide what your highest priorities are and have the courage— pleasantly, smilingly, nonapologetically—to say "no" to other things. And the way you do that is by having a bigger "yes" burning inside. The enemy of the "best" is often the "good."
> – Stephen Covey, *The Seven Habits of Highly Effective People*

The Good and Bad of Checklists

Checklists or To-Do lists are great. I use them all the time. But they aren't sufficient for starting and running a business. You need to go deeper and further than any simple checklist will take you.

Checklists are appropriate for keeping track of simple tasks that have to be completed. They are perfect for shopping lists or for starting to map out a plan of action.

But checklists fail when they become too large or unwieldy. It's hard to establish priorities within a large checklist, or to track dates, sequencing or assignments. That's when it's time to develop a project plan of some kind, whether a simple spreadsheet, an online tool or an advanced software package like Microsoft Project.

Once you develop your project plan, don't stop making checklists! The greatest power in checklists is when they document repeatable processes. Doctors and nurses use them to ensure everything is accounted for before, during and after surgery ("no missing tools left in the patient" kind of stuff). Airline pilots use them to ensure proper safety procedures when flying. And you can use them, too.

Think of any action that you'll be taking on a regular basis. Perhaps it's as simple as posting a new blog entry on your website. A checklist can ensure that you develop a consistent approach. Do you have a catchy title? Did you run spell-check? Are images posted in the proper size and format? Did you add the proper tags and categories? Was it scheduled properly or posted to the site to make it live?

If you can document these checklists for repeatable processes, you've also outlined the first step in outsourcing these kinds of routine tasks. There are many advantages to hiring a personal assistant or virtual assistant. But you'll need to know what work to give them and what results you want before they can help you effectively. Take the time to document your processes, and you'll have a great template to start with.

Evaluation and Daily Celebration/Punishment

When looking through the growing list of things in your plan or on your to-do list, it's important to focus on what needs to be done today. By narrowing your focus to simply working on today's tasks, you can begin to get traction instead of dreaming about or dreading all of the things for the weeks and months ahead.

Begin each week by reviewing your plan. What activities are on the plate for the coming week? Begin to develop a schedule for the week, identifying when you will be working on each task.

Define three to five key actions for each day and then work those to completion.

Whatever method you have, it's important to plan, execute and evaluate daily. At the end of the day or the beginning of the next, look at what was done or left undone from the prior day. Build the daily plan accordingly and get to work.

If you need to, define small rewards or punishments for work that either gets done or doesn't get done. Maybe you can watch a movie that evening if everything gets done...or not, if you don't.

Bad Days

We're all going to have bad days. Those are the days when you look back and realize you've accomplished nothing. Maybe you tried and didn't make any progress. Maybe you just goofed off and look back in shame and regret.

Recognize it as a bad day and move on. My fitness coach, Dr. Steve Berkey of 90Revolutions.com, says that when we miss a day of training we can't make it up. Move on. Pick up where you left off and just keep moving forward.

Are Your Priorities Correct?

How will you know if you're doing the right things, the most important things? Honestly, you may not know at first. It takes time to see which activities produce fruit and which are a waste of time (or at least if it's not the right time yet).

Remember the Plan-Do-Review-Adjust Cycle. Don't overreact and make constant dramatic changes to your plan mid-course. See how things go for a while and make an adjustment if it's needed.

If that part of your plan just isn't working, doesn't seem important anymore, and is sucking the life out of your other projects, kill it, or put it on hold for a while.

Experience and a trusted gut will help some. Having someone you can talk to about it will help a lot! The next chapter deals with that exact point.

Chapter 16:
Don't Go It Alone

No man is an island. DIY is a lie. You can't be good at everything. You need to plug into other people and seek out experts. Good coaching and counsel may cost some time and money, but the return in clarity and action and focus is worth it.

Whether it's the Super Friends, the Justice League, the Avengers or the X-Men... fighting evil is just more fun and effective with a band of brothers and sisters. Invite confidantes into your Fortress of Solitude.

No Man is an Island

There are many things that I like to do by myself. I do a lot of things well and I don't like to ask for help. Yet I cannot maximize my potential if I do everything alone.

I learn when I work with other people or ask someone for help. I save time and get results more quickly and cheaply. Sometimes simply asking is powerful enough to move me forward.

So as much as I want to do things on my own, I know that I cannot do it *all* alone. I need help.

> If I have seen further it is by standing on the shoulders of giants.
> – Isaac Newton, *in a Letter to Robert Hooke, February, 1675 (though the phrase originated with 12th century philosopher Bernard of Chartres... which only enhances the point that no man is an island!)*

DIY is a Lie

There are countless shows and books dedicated to DIY: Do It Yourself. At the surface, this is a good thing. It means that people are learning to do things and growing their minds and abilities.

But what if they didn't have that guide? What if they really had to do it on their own?

Imagine a world where you could only have a car or a house if you could build it yourself.

As Sir Isaac Newton stated, we are standing on the shoulders of giants. I'm glad that someone harnessed fire and invented the wheel, and that others turned that into all of the modern technology we enjoy.

But even standing on someone else's shoulders implies that you're up there alone, doing whatever it is you're doing on your own. The truth is much more complex, because we are tied into communities of people with degrees of interaction and connection that have never been available on our planet before.

Are You Perfect?

I'm a perfectionist at heart, and it is both a blessing and a curse. The blessing comes from my attention to detail and the quality of the things I create. The curse is that the constant pursuit of perfection can keep me from finishing anything because there's always one more thing to be improved.

Note that I'm not saying I'm perfect. Far from it! My perfectionism ensures that I see countless mistakes and errors and imperfections in everything I do. It can be paralyzing at times.

I have to work hard to strike a balance in this part of my personality (remember from Chapter 4...it is listed as both a Strength and a Weakness in my own SWOT diagram).

Admitting that I'm not perfect is a key factor for me to find any level of success. I'm good at seeing my mistakes, but even here I'm not perfect. I still have blind spots. I have to have people around me who can see what I cannot see. They have different skills and abilities and help me immensely. You need them, too!

Admit that you're not perfect. Accept it and then seek out help with your blind spots. When you gain the proper perspective, you can move forward with confidence.

Coaching: The Power of Being Coached

One of the best ways to build up a weak area or take advantage of a Strength is to hire a coach. Find someone with a talent for teaching and helping others achieve the success you want.

The greatest business titans and elite athletes surround themselves with the best coaches. They don't go it alone and they don't rest on their past performance. They strive for constant improvement, knowing that their competition is aiming to unseat them.

When hiring a coach, keep a few key points in mind:

Specific Purpose and Outcome – When you hire a contractor to add an addition onto your home, you don't just tell them to put on an extra room. You have them draw up plans after a consultation. They hear what you want and explain how they can deliver it.

Coaching should work the same way. You have to define the specific outcomes you desire and find a coach who can help you make it happen. I generally don't recommend generic or open-ended coaching. Have a purpose, drive to the outcomes and if additional coaching is needed for another area, continue to get coaching.

Experience If Not Achievement – It seems surprising at first, but many of the greatest sports managers and coaches were not superstar players.

Joe Gibbs, Bill Walsh, Marv Levy, and Bill Parcells never played in the National Football League. In Major League Baseball, Bobby Cox played just two seasons with a .225 career batting average, Tony LaRussa only played 132 games in six seasons with a .199 career batting average, and Joe McCarthy won the World Series seven times as a manager but never played in the pros. Yet they were among the best coaches and managers of all time.

Without a doubt, the superstars work hard, but they also have a natural ability and don't have to work as hard to understand the deeper strategies of the game. My theory is that their natural abilities mask the deeper understanding that someone with less talent has to attain in order to perform at professional levels. That deeper understanding builds the ability to translate it and transfer it to others.

The superstars often struggle to verbalize how they do what they do...they just do it. The same can be true in non-sports coaching (though not always and it depends deeply on the area of coaching). Don't discount a coach who can teach you something with great skill even if they've never performed at the highest echelons of greatness themselves. Their greater talent may be in helping others attain greatness.

Who Works for Whom? – Coaches have different approaches. Some are natural encouragers, while others will get in your face and yell at you. The style of the coach you hire has to work for you and get results for you. Don't take unrelenting abuse (you may have hired a bully) and don't hire someone who never challenges you (you may have hired a wimp).

After a few coaching sessions, you should have a sense of whether or not the coach is the right coach for you. Remember that they work for you...you have the money they want, so make sure you get what you want in return (results!).

And beware of the coach who will work with anyone. They are either desperate or greedy. A true coach is willing to tell a prospect that they are not the right coach for them and can recommend someone else (and a great coach will have a collection of friends and colleagues they can recommend).

The King's Coach

One of the greatest examples of the power of a coaching relationship is the Academy Award-winning movie *The King's Speech*.

It tells the story of King George VI of Britain, who was thrust onto the throne on the eve of World War II. The new king had a very noticeable stammer, and could not project the proper image of a monarch over the radio or in front of crowds.

Prior to his becoming king, his wife encouraged him to see

a speech therapist in the hope that he could overcome the burden of his speech impediment.

I won't give away the movie in case you haven't seen it... but the value here is watching the dynamic relationship between coach and student, especially when the student is royalty! Note the ups and downs throughout the process, the surprising techniques that work (and those that don't), the attitudes that get in the way (pride, shame, etc.), and, of course, the results at the end.

It's one of my favorite movies and reminds me that I need to be coached even though I'm coaching others.

Power of Community

One-on-one coaching for an extended period of time can be very expensive. It's valuable for specific purposes, so don't be afraid to pursue it when needed.

However, if you're on a tight budget or need a more sustained level of support, there are alternatives.

Group coaching can be a great method of getting time with a specific coach while meeting and interacting with other people. Some groups have such high-quality participants that you can learn more from each other than from the coach (which can be a good or bad thing...make sure the coach is engaged and allowing good info to flow through the group, not lazy and unplugged). Group coaching is also an excellent way to find quality contacts to help grow your network.

Another option is to find local or online communities centered on the topics you care about or need help with. One of the greatest I've ever been a part of is the Free Agent Academy (FAA) run by my friend Kevin Miller. I joined as a member and now I'm proud to serve other members as the Roadmap Professor (helping people build plans to implement their business ideas).

FAA is a school for self-employment and personal

development. It features an online community with a semi-structured curriculum that helps members discover their calling and personality, their ideas and branding, and then build plans to market and grow their businesses. Courses are conducted via phone and online, with periodic "intensive" events where members and professors come together for a weekend of hard work and incredible fellowship.

Membership communities like FAA generally have a monthly subscription with additional costs for events or materials. They can have hundreds or thousands of members, allowing you to continue growing your personal network.

Interacting inside a group like this allows you to learn from others who are ahead of you on the journey, and to share your observations with those who are following behind you. You'll also be able to encourage each other in what is often a lonely journey where otherwise well-intentioned friends and family are not so encouraging about your business idea.

> My mentors are those individuals who saw potential in me long before I perceived it in myself – or who challenged me to do more – the people who helped guide me toward excellence.
> – Dr. Benjamin Carson, *Think Big*

Mentoring and Masterminds

Another option for gaining wisdom and advice as you work your plan is to find a mentor or join a Mastermind group.

Mentors are people who are ahead of you on the journey. A new business owner should find a veteran business owner who is successful and willing to help. The types of businesses do not have to be similar, but it can be helpful (though it's not likely if you're in direct competition).

To find a mentor, look around for people or businesses you respect. Seek first to build a relationship…invite them to breakfast or lunch to discuss a specific topic (remember that you pay, okay?). Listen and take notes, gleaning all of the information you can from their experiences. If it goes well and you'd like to make it a regular meeting, ask for a follow-up meeting.

The mentoring relationship can be formal or informal. You may end up mentoring each other mutually, or it could be in the form of a master craftsman and apprentice. What you call it isn't as important as building the relationship with someone who is ahead of you and willing to help. You honor them with your desire to learn, so listen, show respect and follow through.

Mastermind groups are similar to mentoring relationships, but generally involve a larger number of people. These groups are made up of people with similar interests who are willing to get together on a regular basis to share and learn from each other.

There may be existing Mastermind groups that you can join, or you can start one on your own. Look for people who are going somewhere and are serious about continuing to learn and grow. But don't be a leech! You must contribute to the others as you learn from them.

Starting a Board of Advisors

It may also be beneficial to gather a variety of experts who can collectively advise you as you chart the course of your business. The board structure can be formal or informal, but it will probably lean to the informal side in the early phases. It can be structured and run however you see fit, but here are some things to consider:

- **Compensation** – Generally there is little to no compensation involved unless the board is very formal. Do honor your advisors' time and effort appropriately, either with a small gift or at least a thank you card.
- **Variety of Voices** – If you want real advice, you can't have

a bunch of clones on your board. Pick people at different stages of success and life, with different experiences and backgrounds. The variety of perspectives will serve you well.

- **Minimizing Effort/Maximizing Input** – This is not a group that meets weekly or that you interact with frequently. Meet on a regular (perhaps quarterly?) or as-needed basis, but always provide solid information before any gathering. They won't review a 400-page report on your business. Keep it simple and to the point. The SSP can help with that.

- **Don't Give Up Control** – This is not a Board of Directors that has the power to remove you as CEO. They are advising you, but you are in control. They are there to help, but normally do not directly benefit from the success of your company.

- **Use Technology, But Not Exclusively** – In an informal group that's spread across long distances, an online forum or private Facebook group may be the perfect tool to communicate and get different members of the board interacting. But if the opportunity for a face-to-face meeting exists, do it. There is a special energy when people gather for a purpose.

- **Trust is Important** – Don't even think of putting someone on your board if you don't trust them. I don't care if they have tons of connections and influence...it isn't worth it. You must be honest with your board as well. Openly share your plans and your struggles, and be open to their advice. They need to be comfortable sharing their opinions, even if they don't think you'll like what they have to say. You aren't bound to do what they say, but listen respectfully and honestly evaluate their recommendations.

Weekly Accountability

One of the best things I've done for my business efforts is to find an accountability partner. Almost every Friday morning, I wake up early and talk with my friend, Megan Burns. We discuss our accomplishments over the past week, our plans for the coming week, and anything we're struggling with at the moment.

I approached Megan about being accountability partners because I respect what she's done in growing her training and consulting business from scratch (she's the founder/owner of Operations Strategy Consulting—TheOSCedge.com—as well as a new venture for professional women called TheNaptimeCEO.com). We've known each other for several years and simply had a strong connection based on similar backgrounds and experiences.

Look for someone you trust that works in a related but not identical business area (at least not direct competition). It doesn't matter if you are located in the same city or on the other side of the world, as long as you can communicate consistently. You should be different enough in your Strengths and Weaknesses to be able to complement each other.

You both have to bring something to the table. If the relationship is one-sided, it probably won't last very long. It will likely be someone who you've known and perhaps worked with before, not a stranger or new acquaintance. A deep level of mutual respect is required, as is the commitment to make the relationship work. A little "tough love" may be needed from time to time...both of you must be okay with that or no true accountability can take place.

Put a time limit on your weekly meetings or calls, and keep the focus on business. Real life and family relationship issues will pop up (especially if a real friendship exists). That's okay because those things affect your ability to do business. Just don't let the conversation become a weekly chit-chat or gossip session. If it does, refocus on business, end the accountability calls, or just decide to be friends who talk once a week—but don't fool yourself into thinking it's a productive call if it's not.

Outsource Tasks, But Stay in Command

There are three primary reasons to outsource tasks (which can be applied to virtual assistants, independent contractors, vendors and employees):

You're No Good At It – This may seem obvious, and it is. Yet too many people cannot see when they are spending all of their time, energy and resources to accomplish a task with mediocre results. You will get the best results when you spend the majority of your time doing the things you are best at. It's impossible to do it all, all the time. Some tasks have to get done and they land on your plate. But offload the ones you really don't do well.

Do you stink at numbers? Then don't do your own accounting. Not very technical? Don't program your own web site.

Be careful not to ignore these areas once they are outsourced. You have to have a basic understanding or you'll be blindsided by problems or taken advantage of by your help.

Don't Like to Do It – Often there are things we're no good at and we also don't like to do them. Same rules as above apply.

But what about the things that you're good at and don't like to do? Sadly, most people carry these burdensome tasks because they are good at them and have trouble letting go.

Truthfully, you should probably outsource the things you're bad at before you outsource the things you're good at. Just don't hold on to the things you do well but don't enjoy forever. Find someone else to do them or eventually they will rob all of the enjoyment out of your business. You aren't starting this to have a J-O-B. Let go before it's too late.

It's Cheaper Than Doing It Yourself – No matter how good you are at something or how much you love or hate it, there are things you can outsource that don't drive revenue or that free you up to do the things that do. It's your business and you will work the early mornings, late nights, weekends and holidays to make it viable. No one is going to work harder than you are.

Just make sure you work smarter. The hours you spend working in and on your business need to drive the biggest results and biggest profits. This won't be easy in the beginning, but be prepared to move in this direction. Keep it at the top of your mind and always be looking for the tasks you can have someone else do in a cheaper (and perhaps better) way.

What greater wealth is there than to own your life and spend it on growing? Every living thing must grow. It can't stand still. It must grow or perish.

– Ayn Rand, *Atlas Shrugged*
(as said by character Ellis Wyatt)

Chapter 17:
Building a Financial Plan

The difference between running a successful business and a successful hobby is the bottom line. This chapter will show how charting out activity can be translated into a financial model, indicating where readers should focus their energies and perhaps even indicating whether or not a business is viable as envisioned.

Unless you have unlimited resources or can turn coal into diamonds, you'll need to watch the balance sheet as a part of your plan.

The Bottom Line

Rabbi Daniel Lapin, author of one of my favorite books, *Thou Shall Prosper*, says that when someone gives you a dollar, that dollar is simply a certificate of appreciation for a job well done. (If you purchased this book, I thank you for your notes of appreciation!)

If your products or services are helping people and providing value, you can make money.

At the most basic level, profit is a way to keep score in your business. If profits are up, you're doing well. If they aren't, something is wrong.

Unlike the government, no business can stay in operation indefinitely without making a profit (government can't either, but they survive a lot longer and deeper in debt!). You have to make a profit to stay alive. Your profits pay for your house, your food and everything for your family. The more you make, the more you can share, either through growing jobs for others or giving to your church and various charitable organizations.

But if you don't make money, you won't have a business for long. Serve your clients with enough value that they happily hand over their certificates of appreciation.

Before you can think about how many millions of dollars you're going to make, you need to think about what you're going to do to make those millions.

Understand what it is your business is going to do. What are the profit centers (the areas of the business that generate income)? Is there one or are there many that support one another? (I highly recommend having multiple streams of income, so that if one is slow the others can keep your business going).

Multiple Streams of Income

You've no doubt heard the dangers of putting all of your eggs in one basket. The same wisdom applies to running your business. Don't generate all of your income from one source.

In the beginning of your business, it may be that one product or service is your primary offering. That one thing may indeed be your only offering and generate 100% of your revenue. It is rare for a business to stay there and survive.

Look at what you do and find complementary products or services that can shift the burden from one thing to several things.

If you're a writer, your books may be your main thing. But you can give speeches. You can teach classes. You can create workbooks and seminars. There may be tools, software models, subscription websites and any other number of things that your audience is willing to pay for. Let them!

To get a visual representation of this in action, consider your business as a Venn diagram.

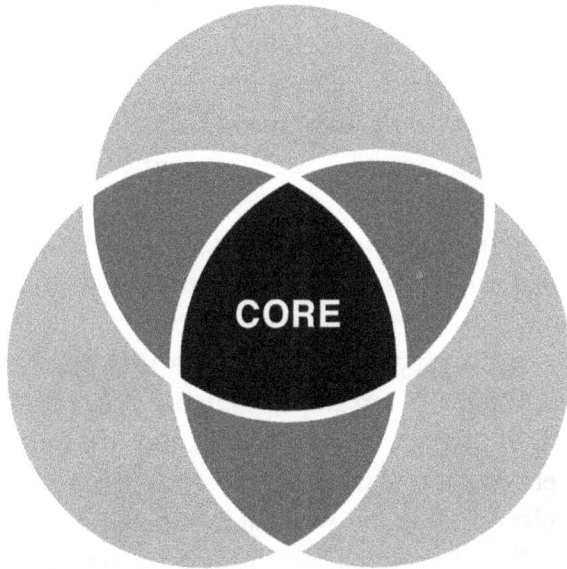

In the center of the diagram is your core product or service. This is the main thing you want to work on and sell.

The other areas overlap the core area. They feed each other and level out the risk of one thing not working out, while helping to pull clients into the other areas.

Examples are all around you if you look for them. The local

running store sells shoes, but they also organize Couch-to-5K classes. Bicycle manufacturers sell bikes, but they also sell all of the equipment and gear that cyclists need, and some also sell exercise vacation packages. Restaurants sell food, but many also have t-shirts and other merchandise for sale. Pick a few businesses and see if you can organize their offerings into the Venn diagram (there may be two, three or more overlapping circles).

Activity-Based Income and Expenses

What are the things you're going to do to run your business? Some will generate revenue directly. This would be true sales and services where you do something and get paid for it. Others are indirect. Perhaps you write a blog or attend networking events. These activities by themselves do not end with cash in your hand, but they introduce you to people who may buy something from you in the future (potential customers).

To do a strong financial forecast, you have to forecast the activities you'll be performing. How many blog posts will you write each month? How many networking events will you attend? How many consultations will you conduct? How many sales calls will you make?

Once you document the activities (these should be in alignment with your action steps), estimate your conversion ratio. If you talk to 10 people about a product and five buy it, you have a 50% conversion ratio. After a few months of results, you'll have a better understanding of what it takes to hit your financial forecast. You'll also see what activities drive revenue, and which ones are a waste of time. Action plus results equals profit.

Conversion Ratios

When you're starting out, estimate low. People don't know you or your product or service, and you probably don't know how to sell it or who to sell it to. With a little practice it should go up and you'll get pretty consistent returns.

If your ratio is too low, try to determine if that is normal for your industry or if it should be higher. Then evaluate what part of your process needs to change in order to get better results.

If your ratio is too high, well, that sounds great, doesn't it? It could be too high because you're not charging enough. If you sell 90% of your customers on a product that costs $10 and you talk to 100 people, you'll make $900. But if you can sell 60% at $20, you'll make $1200. That's the same amount of work but a 25% increase in profit.

Understand how these ratios work to maximize your revenue. Always be thinking about it and experimenting to get the most out of your business. There is no simple, concrete answer except that you want it to be above 0%!

Forecasting Finances

Understanding money in a business is really not that difficult. There are two types of money: Income and Expenses. If your Income exceeds your Expenses, you have Profit. Maximizing Profit is the goal.

Let's look at Expenses first. You will have to spend some money in your business. Expenses can be viewed as Fixed or Variable. A fixed expense is one that doesn't change often. Rent is a fixed expense because it does not go up or down based on the income you generate (you can sell 1 item or 1,000 but your rent is the same). Material costs would be a variable expense. If you have to buy $5 worth of materials to construct your product that you then sell for $10, you have to spend $5 on every item you sell. The price of those materials may fluctuate with the market, or you may be able to get a better price per unit if you order in bulk.

Your total fixed expenses have to be included in the cost of your products or services. If you sell 200 items per month, and have a $200 phone bill, $1 from the sale of each item goes to pay that phone bill. All of your expenses have to be covered by your sales. This is known as a break-even analysis. When expenses are the same as income, you don't make money or lose money. Any additional amount you can charge is profit.

But for profit to exist, value must exist! You can't have outrageous expenses and expect people to pay $100 for a cheese sandwich (unless it's one fine sandwich and you're a killer salesperson!).

Forecasting Integrity

All forecasting is guessing. No one can tell the future, but there are clues you can use to get an idea of how things will be and what actions are most likely to work.

You have to be honest in accounting for your expenses. But even more important is to be honest when forecasting your expenses. If you build a forecast model that looks great by lying to yourself or your business partners, you're setting the table for a big steaming pile of failure.

Your forecasted expenses have to be based on the reality of where you are and your best guess of where things are going to be in the coming months and years. These forecasts help you understand the viability of your business...will it work or not? If it is based on assumptions, write those assumptions down and then drive them to the truth.

Income has to follow the same rules. You have to be honest about it and you need to document your assumptions. When assumptions don't work out, you'll have to make adjustments.

If you have a good idea of the activities you will be performing, you can assign dollar values to the results of those activities. Thus by focusing first on your actions (behavior), you have built a financial model that tells you if it works, or it doesn't.

If it doesn't at first that's okay. Make adjustments to your assumptions, ideas, activities, or finances until it does. If it can't work without ridiculous assumptions or pricing, the business model may be flawed.

This Planning Stuff Works!

The SSP broke my goals down into achievable tasks. This process helped me to understand that the vision God had for me was attainable.

The SSP also helped relieve the financial anxieties starting a new business can bring. It was able to help me to create a realistic budget that correlated my goals with a financial plan to help me develop a viable and thriving organization.

– Rob Coburn, TotalFusionMinistries.org

Does the Business Model Work?

A basic financial forecast when you're starting out will help structure your thought process and identify gaps in your business. It should also show you if your business is viable at all.

If you'll have to work 80-100 hours per week and can only forecast a $10,000/year income, you're better off getting a J-O-B.

But don't quit on your idea just because the first financial projection seems bleak! That just means something needs to change to make it work.

Let's pretend you sell a widget and need to make $100,000 in gross revenue (before all expenses and taxes...never ignore taxes!). You could sell 100,000 widgets to 100,000 people for $1 each. Or you can classify your widget as a luxury/premium product and sell 1,000 widgets to 1,000 people for $100 each.

What if you know your idea is great, but you can't get the numbers to work? Perhaps you need to shift the business model. It could be that you're simply charging for what should be free, and giving away what should cost a lot. Are you selling a product, or an experience? Do you give away DVD players and sell the DVD subscriptions? Do you give away razors, and sell the refill blades? Rethink your business to maximize profit and value.

Forecasting Tools

Unless you are starting a major business or have investors to report to, most business forecasting tools are going to be too advanced and too complicated to use in the beginning of your business. It's more important to do your work instead of learning new software tools and techniques.

However, it is important to gain some level of confidence that your business strategy is viable. A simple spreadsheet (or yellow pad) that lists your assumptions, activities, and business budget will work.

A simple financial forecasting spreadsheet can be downloaded at ConquerYourKryptonite.com. Some people swear by it, others swear at it. Try it and see which kind of person you are.

Chapter 18:
What Price Success? Sacrifice

No one is willing to make a sacrifice if they don't believe it will be worth it. The same is true with your ideas. To make them happen, choices have to be made. Opportunities will have to be passed by, time away from family may be required, and it may cost some money. Is it worth it?

All superheroes have wounds. They make sacrifices in the face of conflict. Not every battle is won. Don't let an unwillingness to sacrifice become your Kryptonite. Victory comes at a cost.

The Will to Sacrifice

No one is willing to make a sacrifice if they don't believe it will be worth it. That doesn't mean we only pursue the sure things, but we do want to be careful with our investments, be it with time or money.

Your ideas are lining up and hoping to be given a chance. Some will get your immediate attention and will come to fruition; some will fail. Some will be ignored forever, while others will be waiting in the wings for years until the time is right.

> There can be no progress, no achievement without sacrifice. A man's worldly success will be in the measure that he sacrifices his confused animal thoughts, and fixes his mind on the development of his plans, and the strengthening of his resolution and self reliance.
> – James Allen, *As a Man Thinketh*

Choosing Between Two Goods

When born, all of your ideas are shiny and new and perfect and full of potential. The luster and excitement for a new idea will wane, sometimes in just minutes. But what do you do when two solid and stable ideas compete with each other? How do you choose?

This is the heart of prioritization. If there is truly no way to execute on both ideas at the same time (a dangerous strategy in most cases), you'll have to make the hard choice and pick one (allowing the other to wait and perhaps die).

Depending on your personality type, this may be very difficult. If you fall in love with ideas, it will be gut-wrenching.

Your ideas are your children and picking between them feels morally wrong. But if you must, evaluate the ideas and make a decision.

A classic approach is to make a list of the pros and cons of each idea. Doing so will often position one idea on top.

Some of the factors you want to consider are:

- Which one will be the easiest to implement to success?
- Will the success of one lead to the opportunity for the other?
- What is the profit potential short-term and long-term for each, and how does that match your timeline needs?
- What does your gut/heart say?
- Spend a few minutes imagining a future pursuing each idea. Which future is more attractive if everything goes according to plan?
- Which idea has a bigger impact on the world or your family?
- Which idea will take the most sacrifice in other areas (financial, family, etc.)?

Rarely are there only two paths forward. If you find yourself in an either/or situation, force yourself to develop 20 approaches instead. They can be radical, crazy and unrealistic (one of mine will invariably involve Elvis or an alien invasion). The point is to get creative and see what else might be possible.

Share your struggle with your community, mentors, and coaches, and let them help. Sometimes talking it out will lead to a clear choice that allows you to move forward with confidence.

Time, Money, Opportunities Lost

Risk is all around us. Do we act today or wait patiently? Realize first that most risk is not as severe as we think it is at the time.

If you tend to be reckless and have the scars to prove it, slow things down just a bit. Contemplating just a few minutes more will give you the information you need to make smarter decisions.

Just don't slow down too much…there's power in your speed of implementation.

If you find yourself hesitating too much, speed up your decision-making process. Recognize that you have scars, too, and they are made of regret and missed opportunities. Don't be foolish, but learn how to make a decision and stick to it. You'll make more mistakes and have some failures, but you'll also get more done and that will outweigh the mistakes and failures.

The Steering Wheel

Remember pretending to drive as a kid? I would get behind the steering wheel in my dad's car and "drive" the highway, moving the wheel left and right constantly.

Later when I learned how to drive in and around Omaha, Nebraska, I realized that the steering wheel doesn't move that much unless you're turning or totally out of control. But it does move, even when driving straight ahead.

With all of the variables working on a moving vehicle—wind, gravity, traction, bumps, etc.—it's nearly impossible to lock the steering wheel in place and still move in a straight line (even in rural Nebraska where the roads are long, flat and straight).

We are constantly moving the steering wheel when we drive, but not with the radical movements of our youthful imagination. Instead the movements are micro-adjustments. We evaluate our position relative to the road and other objects around us, and make the necessary changes to stay on course.

You will need to do the same thing in your business. Keep your hands on the wheel.

Every Second is a Choice

If I asked you where you were going to live ten or twenty years from now, how many possible answers could you think of? Perhaps you plan to stay right where you are, or there are a bunch of places you've always dreamed of living.

But what if I asked you where you were going to live tomorrow? Unless you are on the verge of a move or an unforeseen disaster strikes, you could be pretty sure that you'd be in the same place you are today.

The variable here is time. Given a long period of time, there are more potential choices. With a shorter period of time, the viable options become limited. As time decreases infinitely, there becomes no choice, right?

Then how does anything ever happen? How can we change if we don't insert our existence into the timeline and make something happen by making a choice?

The truth is that we constantly make choices. Often our choice is to keep things exactly as they are. Some circumstances will limit our choices or eliminate the choice of not changing, but we always have a choice.

If we wish to be truly free, we must embrace this concept. No one is responsible for your actions and your choices except you. Go do good stuff and make some great choices. If it doesn't work today, keep choosing and changing until it does.

Commit to the LORD whatever you do, and
He will establish your plans.
  – Proverbs 16:3 (NIV)

FINAL THOUGHTS

Plans change over time. What I hope you get out of this book is a sense of who you are and what you want—and then you can build the plan to make it happen.

The SSP is not magic. It will not do the work for you. But it can help if you let it.

The SSP is also not rigid. Flex it to fit your needs. Change the formatting to reflect what you like best. Add new sections that you think may be helpful. Let me know about them and maybe I'll incorporate them in a new version of this book or share them on my website.

But as you change the SSP, be careful not to remove anything that's important to the process. So add a horn to your bike if you want. It's still a bike. But if you get rid of the chain, it isn't really a bike anymore and it won't take you anywhere.

Visit ConquerYourKryptonite.com to learn more about how I use the SSP and other tools to plan and manage my life and business, including:

- The Simple Strategic Planning Template
- The Simple Financial Forecast Template
- My Weekly and Monthly Calendar Tools
- My Tangible Calendar and more!

Have fun planning and go do good stuff!

James Woosley
james@woosleycoaching.com

ACKNOWLEDGEMENTS

There are so many people whom I have to thank for being a part of my life and therefore a part of this book. I know that as soon as I complete the final proof, I'll remember one more. I guess that's what second editions are for.

We all need a Gandalf—someone who steps into and disrupts our comfortable lives because he sees more in us than we see in ourselves. He sets us on a new path—a challenging adventure that was in us all along, but one that we would never enter into without a push. Chuck Bowen is my Gandalf. Thank you.

I have to thank my wife Heather and our kids, Anna and Ian. You are the reason for my plans in life.

Thanks also to my mother and father (Barry and Elaine), brother and sister (John and Pamela), grandparents, aunts, uncles, cousins, in-laws, outlaws and everyone else in my beautiful and crazy family.

To my brothers and sisters in the United States Armed Forces—it was my greatest honor to serve in your ranks. Your uniforms are not costumes, but you are the truest Superheroes the world has ever known.

To the teachers and educators who took the time to invest in me outside of and beyond the classroom—it's amazing how many of you told me to reach for the stars. Miss Dorsey, Miss Clevenger, Lt. Col. Tosti, Chief Jones, Chief Stohlman, SMSgt Gerbus, Mrs. Beckstead—and many, many others—thanks to you, I've touched them.

And to the modern writers and visionaries like Zig Ziglar, Dave Ramsey, Dan Miller, Seth Godin, John G. Miller, Ari Weinzweig, Steven Pressfield, Rabbi Daniel Lapin, Andy Andrews, and so many others—thank you for igniting the sparks I used to change my mindset and my life...I'm on fire now and it's great!

To the founders of Free Agent Academy, Kevin Miller and Chuck Bowen, as well as my fellow professors and leaders there—I'm on this journey because of your support and encouragement over the last four years. I would be stuck if not for you:

Gary Barkalow	Alan Jackson
Christopher Browning	Deb Ingino
Rona Davis	Justin Lukasavige
Brenda Dunagan	Pierce Marrs
Kevin Gainey	Teri Miller
James Garner	Jonathan Pool
Jimi Gibson	Andy Traub

To Kent Julian and the members of his Speak It Forward Coaching and Mastermind Program, who've watched this book go from a comment to a dream to a reality—thank you for sticking with me so long!:

Megan Burns	Andy Perkins
Matthew Casteel	Trent Thomas
Rob Clinton	Lynne Watts
Jesse Lahey	Kimberley Wiggins
Guy Madison	

To George Amequito for the stunning book cover—it's a cover I'll always be proud to have displayed in my office. And as if that wasn't good enough, you crafted almost every other logo and graphic for the book and website. Above and beyond!

To Jennifer Harshman, who killed the double-spaces after my periods, fixed my dangling ~~adverbs~~ participles, and generally brought more active voice to the text—any errors that remain are the ones I decided to keep or that I added after your review.

To Kerry Kruegler, for the great headshot and other pictures from an almost rainy day in Atlanta—I appreciate your patience, excitement, and willingness to do whatever it takes to get the right shot!

And to the members of my book team, who offered feedback and advice, who held my feet to the fire, and who helped promote this collection of words to the masses—thank you! We did it!

George Amequito	Erin Johnstone
Toni Amequito	Mark Jones
Robert Bartlett	Melodie Kenniebrew
Susanne Ballard	Jesse Lahey
Chuck Bowen	John O. McKee
Jody Berkey	Sue McLuen
Steve Berkey	Kevin Miller
Henry Brown	Kay Powell
Megan Burns	Steven Samry
Rob Clinton	Eric Schram
David Creel	Jason Smith
Rona Davis	Vanessa Stewart
Tony Elam	Celia Triplett
Julia Gray-Lion	Jana Hoggle
Dennis Hanson	Christopher Vicente
Jennifer Harshman	Lynne Watts
Amber Hendrickson	Kimberley Wiggins
Michael Hollingsworth	Archie Winningham
Alan Jackson	Heather Woosley

However, I am NOT thanking Scott Wood. His bad advice served only for comic relief. And I think he really wanted me to write a book about zombies. Maybe next time, buddy!

THIS ISN'T THE END... IT'S THE BEGINNING!

This is my life purpose statement:

"I communicate the potential I see
in a way that can be realized."

It took me a long time to put those words together. It happened during my LifePlan on a snowy day in Michigan when Jonathan Pool—my friend and one of my personal coaches—pulled them out of me. Just 13 simple words that connect everything my life was, is, and will be.

Woosley Coaching exists to empower, equip, and encourage life and business transformation in the areas of planning and strategy, allowing clients to advance boldly in the direction of their dreams and goals.

I live out my life purpose by helping others become more than they see in themselves. I hope the book has helped you, and I'd love to help some more.

Please visit WoosleyCoaching.com to sign up for my newsletter. While you're there, read the blog and continue learning how to get more out of your plans.

If you'd like to work with me directly, I offer a variety of tools and coaching packages including:

- SSP Review and Feedback
- Courses/Seminars/Coaching Groups
- One-on-One and Executive Coaching
- StratOp Facilitation

I'm also available to speak to your organization or conduct onsite training courses.

Did CtEK Make an Impact?

Think back on what you learned as you read *Conquer the Entrepreneur's Kryptonite*. Write down one thing you learned that needs immediate action:

If you can do that, then please say this to your friends:

"You have got to read this book..."

Write down the names of three people you are going to recommend this book to:

1) _____

2) _____

3) _____

Lend these people your book or buy them a copy.

At least share a link to ConquerYourKryptonite.com so they can buy their own copy!

Pass It Around List

Write down your name and the date you finished reading the book:

Loan this book to a friend or give it away with the promise that they do the same. Each person can then add their name to the list below:

	Name	Date
1		
2		
3		
4		
5		
6		
7		
8		
9		
10		
11		
12		
13		
14		
15		
16		
17		
18		

ConquerYourKryptonite.com

www.ingramcontent.com/pod-product-compliance
Lightning Source LLC
Chambersburg PA
CBHW071725200326
41519CB00021BC/6568